click

click

What We Do Online
and Why It Matters

BILL TANCER

HarperCollins*Publishers*

HarperCollins*Publishers*
77–85 Fulham Palace Road,
Hammersmith, London W6 8JB
www.harpercollins.co.uk

First published in the USA by Hyperion 2008
First published in the UK by HarperCollins*Publishers* 2009

1 3 5 7 9 10 8 6 4 2

A catalogue record of this book is
available from the British Library

ISBN   978-0-00-727783-4

Printed and bound in Great Britain by
Clays Ltd, St Ives plc

Mixed Sources
Product group from well-managed
forests and other controlled sources
www.fsc.org   Cert no. SW-COC-1806
© 1996 Forest Stewardship Council

FSC is a non-profit international organization established to promote
the responsible management of the world's forests. Products carrying
the FSC label are independently certified to assure consumers that they
come from forests that are managed to meet the social, economic
and ecological needs of present and future generations.

Find out more about HarperCollins and the environment at
www.harpercollins.co.uk/green

CONTENTS

Acknowlededgments xi

Introduction 1

PART I: UNDERSTANDING OURSELVES 15

Chapter 1: PPC – Porn, Pills and Casinos 17

Our fascination with skin, quick fixes and easy money. Actions speak louder than words, as aggregate interaction with the underbelly of the Internet reveals patterns that aren't easy to ascertain from traditional sources.

Chapter 2: Getting to What We Really Think 45

Do platform stand, voting record and integrity determine whom we vote for? Search-term data reveals a lot about a candidate's brand and the half-life of negative information. See how these insights may innovate the way we measure brand in the business world.

Chapter 3: Prom in January 69

Why do searches for 'prom dresses' peak in the first week of January? Internet searches reveal that our gut instincts regarding seasonality are often wrong, resulting in market inefficiencies. We have much to learn from consumers; we just have to observe collective search patterns.

Chapter 4: Failed Resolutions
and the False Hope Syndrome 97

Our commitment to New Year change is surprisingly
short-lived, with 'diet' searches lasting less than a week. Outrageous claims as to how we can improve ourselves with no effort
lead ultimately to the downward spiral of false hope.

Chapter 5: Celebrity Worship Syndrome 121

The Internet and specifically celebrity blogs have brought
unprecedented public access to the lives of celebrities, fuelling
our obsession with the famous.

Chapter 6: What Are You Afraid Of?
and Other Telling Questions 141

We search on information about our fears – over 1,000 unique
ones – from fear of public speaking to fear of elbows and ceiling
fans. Search engines have become a new non-judgemental place
for us to ask questions we are increasingly less likely to ask each
other.

Chapter 7: Web Who.0 167

Is the 80/20 rule passé? With all the hype around Web 2.0,
surprisingly few Internet users actively create
consumer-generated media, giving rise to the new 1-9-90 rule.

**PART II: WHAT'S POSSIBLE
WITH WHAT WE KNOW 195**

Chapter 8: Data Rocks and the
Television–Internet Connection 197

Laptops have become increasingly popular in the living room.
Our Internet behaviour reveals how we react online to what we
see on the tube. As the television–Internet gap closes, we learn
what motivates us to interact.

Chapter 9: Women Wrestlers and
Arbitraging Financial Markets 217

Does volume of search terms translate to popularity? Is it
possible to predict reality television show votes from how
Internet users search? Near real-time Internet data provides a
time advantage over traditional leading economic indicators.

Chapter 10: Finding the Early Adopters 239

New technology spreads through society in predictable
segments, starting with Innovators and Early Adopters. Internet
behaviour viewed in the correct light can help illuminate who the
Early Adopters are and what they're doing today.

Chapter 11: Super-Connectors and
Predicting the Next Rock Star 259

Visitors to official band websites traditionally come from either
social networks or search engines; graphing these two sources of
traffic allows us to visualize Malcolm Gladwell's 'tipping point'.

Epilogue: Who We Are and Why It Matters 279
Notes 287
Glossary 295
Index 297

For Lori

ACKNOWLEDGEMENTS

If you looked around our house, you'd quickly discover my obsession with books. Much to my wife's consternation (although she has her own collection), there are books everywhere – on the bookshelves where they belong, on the bedside table, in the kitchen, stacked in the corners on every available surface. I love books, but the process of writing *Click* has made me realize that in my voracious consumption of printed text I've really taken books for granted. I had no idea just how many talented individuals are required to take something from concept to finished product. It takes a village to write a book.

Click is based on my work at Hitwise. It's hard for me to think of Hitwise as a company; I consider my colleagues to be part of my extended family, spread over four continents. I was very fortunate to have Tessa Court as my internal champion at Hitwise, but equally fortunate to work with Andrew Walsh and Chris Maher in making this book a reality. I owe deep gratitude to Hitwise analysts, both past and present: Heather Hopkins, who inspired the "tipping point" chapter; LeeAnn Prescott, who first discovered the prom dress phenomenon; as well as Robin Goad, Heather Dougherty, Sandra Hanchard and Eva Stringleman, who served as never-ending sources of inspiration; and a special thanks to our head of media relations, Matt Tatham, for helping to get the word out.

This project would never have left the concept stage had it not been for my good fortune in landing one of the most talented literary agents on the planet, Melissa Flashman with Trident Media Group. Melissa's excitement about *Click* was both electric and contagious. As a first-time author, I hit the jackpot in landing Mel as my agent.

I knew we had found the right home for *Click* at Hyperion. Many thanks to Bob Miller and Ellen Archer for enthusiastically embracing the book's concept and championing what I had to say. Thanks to Gretchen Young for her thoughtful and considerate work in guiding me in the right direction, to Beth

Gebhard and Alex Ramstrum for lining up amazing publicity, and to Jane Comins and Sarah Rucker and her team. Rick Willett, who provided copy-edits for *Click*, deserves special recognition for the tedium of correcting my grammar and spelling and turning the manuscript into something readable. Thanks also to Elizabeth Sabo, who served as my lifeline to the Hyperion team.

Sitting in Jonathan Taylor's office at HarperCollins UK, I knew that my luck in drawing the best in publishing had crossed the pond. Jonathan's enthusiasm for *Click* UK was truly contagious. I am also indebted to Steven Burdett, my project editor, Colin Hall for expert typesetting, Kay Carroll, *Click*'s production manager, and Jane Beaton in Publicity.

Of course there are the friends who stood by me throughout the book-writing process and those whom I met along the way. Thanks to my office neighbour and lunch buddy Luke McGuiness, who was always a willing sounding board. I credit Rafael Zorrilla with coming up with the chapter title for the book's first chapter. PPC means something in online marketing-speak, but Rafael has his own definition, which I borrowed with his permission. Thanks also to Daisy Whitney for her inspiration and comic relief in the book-writing process, and thanks to the Roosters (Bill, Jim, John, Bruce, Norm, Tim and

Gregg), my Saturday bike group, for letting me ride in the back of the group so that I could think about what I was going to write next.

I can't forget the wonderful support of my family. To my parents, Marty and Sheila Tancer, who always supported and encouraged me in all of my endeavours, and to my mother-in-law, Paulette Minden, whose optimism for *Click* was a constant source of inspiration.

Finally, as I finished *Click* it occurred to me that there really should be a support group for spouses/significant others of writers. My amazing wife, Lori, to whom I've dedicated this book, didn't flinch when I sat her down and announced that I was going to write a book (to appreciate this you'd have to consider all the previous half-baked ideas I had announced in the past). Throughout the writing process, Lori has been there for me, has put up with the moodiness that can go along with writing, not to mention the endless conversations and questions about prom dresses, and when needed has served as drill sergeant when I was just too tired to continue. Thanks for always being there, and for giving me the inspiration and support that helped make *Click* a reality.

PREFACE

As I walked into the meeting area of the Central London Hotel I immediately noticed that there was a different vibe here compared to the countless convention spaces that I've visited in the United States.

It was quiet, somber and very intense.

When I've had the pleasure of presenting at a search conference in the states, there's a noticeable din as you approach the conference floor. On this particular morning, conference attendees were sitting on the floor or standing up against the wall, all thumbing through a search engine report authored by our UK analyst Heather Hopkins. People were studying every chart, table and data point in the report, no doubt searching for an explanation as to why this search engine had increased its share whilst another had fallen in rank.

On that morning I added another difference between online marketers in the US and the UK to my list. There was a clear 'got-it' factor and an equally noticeable hunger for data surrounding our online habits. Throughout my five years studying the Hitwise database in various countries, I've always been fascinated by the similarities and differences in our culture as evidenced by what we do online.

You don't have to search very far to find differences in search patterns between Americans and Brits. In the US 'how to tie a tie' is the number one 'how to' query for the last three years running without fail. In the UK, the last time I ran the data, that same search ranked 51 amongst 'how to' searches.

Similarities are equally if not more intriguing. From prom dresses (Chapter Three) to our online fascination with reality television shows like *Strictly Come Dancing* (Chapter Nine), our online habits reveal a common thread that can span continents and oceans.

Click hit the bookshelves in September 2008, the week after Sarah Palin was named on the Republican ticket for the US presidential election. In the months following the US release another similarity surfaced between our samples in the Asia Pacific region, the UK and North America: every market became obsessed with the celebrity of America's next leader and 'hot photos' of the Republican running mate. Chapter Two of this UK edition is updated with observations from this unprecedented contest.

Having access to the aggregate search behaviour of over 25-million Internet users worldwide (8.4 million here in the UK alone) provides limitless insights into what affects us and ultimately who we are. I hope you find the insights in Click as intriguing as I have.

Enjoy,

Bill Tancer

INTRODUCTION

On my way in to work in San Francisco from our house in San Mateo, something about the radio interview I was listening to just didn't sound right. The reporter was talking to a British psychologist about the third week in January, a week that he claimed was the most depressing week of the year. The interviewee detailed how he had reached that conclusion from a mathematical formula he'd developed that factored in failed New Year's resolutions, credit card debt from the holidays, and weather patterns. All factors taken together pointed to the third week in January as the most depressing of the year. It sounded like a convincing story; I just had a hard time believing it.

While I'm all in favour of mathematical formulae, was it possible to build one that would detect a society's swing towards depression? You probably couldn't even detect such a thing by surveying a large sample of the population – can we count on people to answer questions about depression honestly? No, I was having trouble buying this story because I had just charted 'depression' a few weeks earlier and I knew that the most depressing week of the year occurred right around Thanksgiving. How did I know that?

Pulling from a sample of 10 million Internet users in the United States, I was interested in seeing when people search for the term 'depression'. My thought process was as follows: If as a society we become more depressed during certain parts of the year, a certain percentage of us, in order to seek help, will turn to our nearest confidant, a place we can go to and ask questions without fear of being judged. We will search on Google, Yahoo! Search or MSN Search.

My first chart of the term, over a two-year period of time, didn't quite add up. It showed a pattern that seemed to reflect the school calendar. This was probably due to the fact that schoolchildren were using search engines for research papers about the Great Depression. Not to be deterred, I created a new chart, this time combining the volume of searches for common antidepressants, drugs like Zoloft, Cymbalta, Lexapro. The pattern was pretty clear, once you ruled out the Great Depression and factored in pharmaceuticals: A significant number of us turned to our search engines in the week of Thanksgiving in the hope of understanding our holiday blues.

This morning's drive was pretty typical for me. I hear things on the news, read items in the newspaper or catch snippets of discussions among fellow workers, and I have a burning urge to run to my computer and see if I can shed light on the topic du jour based on our Internet searches or visits to particular websites. Sometimes random associations just pop into my head and I turn to search-term data to see if there is any relationship. These ventures into data serendipity have led to some very interesting questions, from why prom dresses spike in January to the connection between women wrestlers and the arbitrage of financial indicators. What day of the week is the most popular for visits to pornographic websites? What scares us most? What questions are on our minds? How are new Web 2.0 sites creating society's new winners and losers?

The answers to these questions and many more like them can be found in a massive database of Internet behaviour. I spend my days (and many of my nights) deep in the recesses of this data. When I can't sleep, I find myself sifting through traffic charts, tables of searches, demographics and psychographics, turning the different pieces of data around in my head, examining them from different angles.

What struck me at first as just a lot of data is actually something much greater. If you spend enough time considering all the different elements of our Internet use, you begin to compile an ever clearer picture of who we are and what exactly is on our minds. The 'who' that I'm referring to is a sample of more than 10 million Internet users in the United States, and the database is an anonymized and aggregate collection of what this massive group of Internet users do online every day. The 'what' is a company called Hitwise. I work as the general manager of global research for the company.

Sometimes I have a hard time remembering exactly what I did before working for Hitwise. But I do remember how one phone call, a sales call from Chris Maher, who at the time was the general manager of the US market for the company, and was later to become the company's president, changed the course of my career. This one call would drive me to switch to a job that provided me with such rich data, I would quickly find myself in the executive suites of some leading companies in the United States and abroad, and I would be invited to lecture at top universities, give keynotes at industry events, author a weekly online column for *TIME,* and eventually write this book. Of course I didn't know that my ringing phone would lead to such a major life change; at the time I was annoyed that my concentration had been broken by the telephone ringing on my desk.

I was busy working for the head of sales and business development at my current employer, Look-Smart, a search engine that employed a large team of editors to inject human input into search results. As the head of market research, I was troubled by one massive project that had landed in my lap.

As a search engine, LookSmart derived its revenue from advertisers who wanted their advertisements to show up when consumers entered a particular word in our search box. So if I were in the business of selling Waterford crystal, when a consumer searched for this particular term, or maybe just the term 'crystal', I would want an ad for my online crystal store to show up within the listings, with the hope that a searcher might click on it and eventually buy crystal from my online shop. To accomplish this, I would enter into an agreement with LookSmart to pay a small fee, maybe $0.10, when anyone clicked on my Waterford crystal ad on the LookSmart search results page.

From a sales perspective, there was a big problem with this business model. The LookSmart sales force (or really, the sales force of any search engine at the time) had no clue how much inventory they had of searches for a particular phrase, such as 'Waterford crystal' or 'crystal'. This problem meant that our sales force was essentially selling blind. They could waste days, weeks or months selling a search campaign to an advertiser, only to learn that nobody was actually searching for the terms that the advertiser was interested in.

As we sat in the café portion of the LookSmart building, an old converted warehouse on Second Street in San Francisco (big open-beamed space reminiscent of the Dot Com era), Robert Goldberg, who headed up sales and business development for Look-Smart at the time, explained the problem this way: 'I have a sales team that's selling inventory from a warehouse, but there's no reporting system to tell me what's in the warehouse; there's not even a door or window into this warehouse – we're just forced to guess what's inside.' Imagine running a sales organization with absolutely no visibility into what you are selling. The potential for inefficiency is enormous.

We did have one set of data, which Robert had delivered to my desk on a CD-ROM (the file was huge): a sample of our biggest set of inventory at the time, one week's worth of searches on Microsoft's MSN Search engine. This one slice of search activity, for one week out of one year, contained a staggering 40 million search terms. Somehow from this massive file of terms I had to find a way to estimate what our inventory of retail terms was – how many searches there were for different models of cars, what people typed into a search engine when they were trying to navigate to an online dating service, and on and on. An hour had gone by and I hadn't moved from my computer screen, scrolling through a sample of the top 10,000 terms, which I had downloaded into Excel.

The call from Hitwise came at what I thought was the worst possible time, but it turned out to be just the right time. I had to get back to Robert with my ideas on estimating our search inventory and didn't have time to listen to a sales pitch. I apologized to Chris and we scheduled a call for the next day. But before he hung up Chris asked about some of the challenges I was facing at LookSmart. Out of my desperation for answers I decided to let my new acquaintance in on the problem, but only by giving him a small piece of the puzzle. 'I'm trying to estimate the amount of interest in the wedding sector,' I said. (If I was going to have to listen to a sales pitch, maybe I could get something out of it!)

The next day I received a forty-five-page Power-Point deck long in advance of our call (not a good sign), and I purposefully blocked off only thirty minutes for the call in case I needed to escape.

They had me by the second slide. At that time my external sources of data were based on what I thought were large samples, between 40,000 and 100,000 Internet users in the United States. On the second slide of the deck, the data I was looking at was based on a sample of more than 10 million Internet users. This was unbelievable. So much so that I wasn't sure if I did believe it.

A thought immediately struck me; I was trying to solve my problem of estimating inventory by looking at one week's worth of data, when the chart in front of me clearly demonstrated just how seasonal Internet activity can be. Wedding site traffic spikes predictably during the summer months (wedding season), but looking closer at patterns in wedding-related search terms, like 'wedding dresses', shows a very different pattern, with spikes in searches occurring during the first weeks of the year. Aggregate search behaviour could show us when consumer demand peaks for various goods and services. I was hooked.

Convincing my boss was a different matter. When I explained how this new vendor's data could provide us with granular detail on all of the top US sites, he didn't think it was real. In order to convince him of the data's accuracy, I devised a plan. Since we controlled the main results for MSN's search engine, we had a fair amount of control over the amount of search traffic that a site might receive from MSN. During two days in November, as a test, we placed a site called TripAdvisor (which was small at the time) into the top position in MSN results. Without revealing the dates, I asked Chris to chart the traffic for TripAdvisor over several months. We agreed that if he could pinpoint the two days using Hitwise's data, he had a new customer. Five minutes later the chart came through, and sure enough he had nailed the exact days.

After signing the contract, as I began using Hitwise data at LookSmart, I found myself facing a dilemma. I now had at my fingertips a looking glass into the aggregate Internet behaviour of one of the largest samples in existence. At the time I could study more than 500,000 websites in 164 different industry categories, and have the data updated every day with new information. I suffered briefly from analysis paralysis as I tried to figure out where to start in this database. But that didn't last very long. I quickly realized that insight lay everywhere, from measuring the effectiveness of a competitor's marketing plan to assessing interest in a yet-to-be-released movie by determining the amount of traffic visiting an official movie site.

I found myself losing track of time, spending hours finding interesting facets in the data, serendipitously following paths to counterintuitive conclusions. I didn't have enough time for my actual job. It was at this point that I approached Hitwise about the idea of working for them full-time as the head of research, an evangelist to show other users how to use this amazing trove of data, and to educate the market in general about the value of online competitive intelligence.

ABOUT THE DATA

The stories and examples in this book are based on data gathered from the Hitwise Competitive Intelligence Service. Unless otherwise specified, I relied on the US sample. (Hitwise captures data in the United States, the UK, Hong Kong, Singapore, Australia, and New Zealand.) The US sample contains the usage behaviour of more than 10 million Internet users. The sample is gathered in two ways. The primary methodology, based on agreements with multiple ISPs throughout the country, anonymizes and aggregates usage data on more than 7.5 million users. The data is gathered from a number of ISPs to get a cross-section of Internet users regionally. The ISP sample is supplemented with multiple opt-in panels, or groups of Internet users who have agreed to be monitored and have supplied demographic information. That information allows us to report on the demographic and psychographic profiles of visitors to various sites and categories of sites. Both the ISP and opt-in data update every day, providing usage information for the previous day; search-term data is updated on a weekly basis; and demographic and psychographic data are based on a four-week rolling average of usage.

ABOUT PRIVACY

When I first show a friend, journalist or business prospect the data that we have access to, one of the questions that commonly arises is: What about user privacy? Isn't the data that we're gathering a violation of end-user privacy? As a business, we know it's in our best interests to protect the privacy of end-users. We accomplish this through several mechanisms. First, our ISP and opt-in data partners anonymize and aggregate the data that is sent over to our system to analyse. In other words, we can't track any of our data back to individual Internet users (nor would we want to). We're more interested in tracking overall trends and gathering insights into how Internet users in aggregate are using the Web. We also scrub our search-term data to remove any personally identifiable information (phone numbers, credit card numbers, Social Security numbers and so on).

ABOUT THE BOOK

This book is presented in two key sections. In Part I you'll get to ride along as we explore fascinating points of data that have come up over the years. From visiting the dark side of the Internet and our habits revolving around porn, pills and casinos, to understanding our obsession with celebrity, you'll see how our Internet behaviour sheds light on why we do the things we do. We'll talk about the questions that we pose to search engines and what they reveal about us, such as queries about our fears, things that we would like to learn to do, or just general questions like 'Why is the sky blue?' We will also address how some of the latest innovations in Internet communications have changed the way we interact with one another.

In the second half of the book we'll explore both actual and theoretical uses of this data, from the tactical applications that define the industry of online competitive intelligence, to the exciting potential to use the data to identify hot Internet trends, even to predict the next big rock star.

The most suitable place to start our journey

through Internet behaviour has to be the underbelly of the Net. In the world of Internet marketing, the acronym PPC stands for 'pay per click', the business model that addresses how much a business would be willing to pay for the users who clicked on their search advertisement. In my world, however, and in Chapter 1, PPC also has a different definition: It refers to porn, pills and casinos. Internet data that surrounds our vices demonstrates just how compelling competitive intelligence data can be, from understanding the ebb and flow of traffic to websites, to discovering who visits those sites and what exactly is behind their decision to visit.

1

UNDERSTANDING OURSELVES

CHAPTER 1

PPC – Porn, Pills and Casinos

I n 2006 the federal government declared that the Internet was 99 per cent porn-free, based on a study conducted by Professor Philip Stark of UC Berkeley. The study examined sites indexed by Google and Microsoft and found that only 1 per cent of those sites were pornographic. Yet, on the other side of the spectrum, some studies have put pornographic Web visits as high as 40 per cent of all online activity. With such a wide variance of results, where along the spectrum does the true answer exist?

When we greet old friends, it's customary to say how great someone looks (regardless of the person's actual appearance). Partly as a result of societal norms and partly due to our desire to make ourselves and others feel good, we don't always say how we really feel. When we catch a child reaching into a biscuit tin when he knows he's not supposed to, we know there's a good chance that if we ask the question 'What are you doing?' we'll get an answer that contradicts actual observed behaviour. The story of the underbelly of the Internet, our online vices, starts here, with our capacity to deny the truth. Sometimes we say what we mean, and sometimes we don't, but actions always speak louder than words.

Sex sells. And sometimes sex can get stolen. Just ask Gary Kremen.

I first met Gary when I was working as the head of research for LookSmart. Gary had come by the office to explore a potential relationship between our company and one of his ventures, Galaxy Search, a search engine that catered to the adult industry. LookSmart, like all search engines, had an inventory of adult-related search terms. (By 'inventory' I'm referring to a quantity of searches entered by consumers who crossed our servers.)

I was a little tentative entering the meeting. We hadn't entertained the idea of offloading our adult searches before, and throughout my career I had heard horror stories about dealing with the adult industry, legal and bad-debt issues primarily. The situation was complicated by the fact that the conference room next to ours was occupied by the owners of a parental control software program that was in the early stages of potential acquisition by LookSmart. (The parental control executives were rumoured to be fairly religious.) Needless to say, our neighbours weren't big fans of the adult industry (or perhaps they were, since without porn their business would be non-existent).

Early in the meeting, Gary proceeded to tell me about his foray into adult content on the Web, specifically about his ownership and the eventual theft of the domain sex.com. In the early 1990s, Gary, a self-employed software salesman, had been a pioneer in the domain-name squatting business (the practice of registering multiple Internet domain names in the hope of selling those names in the future or capitalizing on traffic visiting those addresses). Gary had had some early success, buying up domain names such as jobs.com, autos.com and housing.com, to name a few.

While he went on to found the industry-leading Match.com, originally an email-based dating service that he purchased for $2,500 in 1994 (and for which he later received a paltry sum of only $50,000 and a lifetime membership on the site),[1] Gary's most valuable asset was one of those domains that he registered in 1994 – sex.com.

In 1995, while reviewing records of his Internet

properties, Gary was shocked to learn that he was no longer listed as the owner of the sex.com domain. The property that would prove to be his most valuable asset was now in the hands of an unsavoury character by the name of Stephen Michael Cohen.

Kremen launched into a legal battle lasting more than ten years that included a $65 million court judgment. Kremen's legal team documented that Cohen had made in excess of $750,000 a month in pay-per-click revenue from the stolen domain name.[2] Sex.com, at the time, was referred to as a parked domain, or a site that has no original content but does contain paid links to other sites. Many Internet users, in the hopes of finding prurient content, click on these paid links, which generates income for the site owner. In 2001 Kremen was awarded Cohen's 9,800-square-foot Spanish-style residence in Rancho Santa Fe, complete with tennis and volleyball courts.

Kremen has since sold his legally recouped domain name back to Cohen for $12 million and additional properties of Cohen's, including two parcels of Tijuana property and a shrimp farm and strip club in Mexico. This protracted legal fight, which spanned a decade, involving revenues that exceeded $100,000,000, all stemmed from a simple domain name that included no special content ... just a simple Web address that was able to generate a fortune in Internet advertising dollars based on Internet users' quest for sex.[3]

As the meeting wrapped up, Gary mentioned his infamous sex.com party, which he was having at his Rancho Santa Fe house the following week, and suggested that we fly down to Southern California to check it out. A quick image flashed through my mind, as I played out telling my wife that I had to fly down to Rancho Santa Fe to go to the sex.com party. My mental assessment of the situation was that there was virtually no chance I'd be on a plane to San Diego the following week.

As I walked Gary to the lift, I began thinking about how one little domain name could generate so much cash, with virtually no content except paid links. If this were any indication, the revenue generated by the online adult industry would have to be massive. As I walked back to my cube, I wondered what data I might be able to pull to estimate the revenue potential of the industry. I knew hard data would be difficult to come by.

MY DESK WAS A cluttered mess, filled with print-outs of different industry figures, growth rates, advertising spending, etc. . . . All of this information lived in my email and was bookmarked in my Web browser, but I'm very tactile when it comes to data, often finding inspiration in the notes I write in the margins of these various reports. While I hadn't come across many industry figures for online adult entertainment, there was one study that estimated the sector at $97 billion a year. Some claim that this figure is wildly overblown, while others report that the number under-reports the actual revenues derived from adult content. One of the confounding issues in estimating the size of the adult industry is getting an accurate read on porn consumption. There are two potential sources to inform this market sizing: what adult industry vendors report as their revenue, and how often consumers say they visit the sites.

Starting with the porn producers, is that a source to be trusted? Nothing against them; in fact in research it's a widely accepted fact that using one side of the equation to estimate a market is not sound, especially if one side has an incentive to make their numbers appear bigger. In this case, it would clearly be within producers' interest to over-report their revenues, potentially attracting more investment and greater advertising dollars to the sector. On the other hand, you could turn to the demand side and ask adult entertainment consumers, but this is even more troubling.

Imagine fielding the consumer survey aimed at estimating true porn consumption. Maybe it would go something like this: The phone rings, perhaps at seven-thirty in the evening, just as your interview subject is sitting down to dinner. 'Hello, I'm conducting a survey on behalf of — market research firm. Would you be willing to answer some questions about your interest in online pornography?' This hypothetical interruption to your subject's evening poses two problems: (1) Who would be willing to take such a survey? and (2) Could we trust the answers that the subject provided us with?

In the age of do-not-call lists, voice mail and ever-increasing wariness of strangers, it's becoming more and more difficult for research firms to include a representative set of survey respondents in their studies. Busy young professionals and savvy and distrustful consumers are opting out of participating in these projects, leaving researchers with data only from older, more willing subjects. Even though the do-not-call list does not apply to market research, the advent of 'the list' has left consumers feeling more empowered when fielding unwelcome telephone calls. The end result is research based on a subset of our population rather than a well-rounded sample.

The second issue is even more critical. As participants in surveys, most of us tend to want to cast ourselves in as positive a light as possible; we don't want to provide insight into our daily lives that might make us look unsavoury. Posing questions about the consumption of adult material online would be a worst-case scenario for any researcher. The problem lies in the concept of cognitive dissonance.

Leon Festinger, a Stanford professor specializing in social psychology, first explored the theory of cognitive dissonance in 1957, after the publication of his book *When Prophecy Fails*. In his book, Festinger discussed the beliefs of a doomsday cult that thought the world was coming to an end at the hands of some extraterrestrial beings. When the prophecy failed, cult members were struck by dissonance; they had been brainwashed to believe that the world was coming to an end, yet the date had passed and the world was still in existence. Most members of the cult resolved this dissonance by reasoning that the aliens had decided to spare their world, because of the devotion that the cult members had shown to their cause.

A failed apocalyptical alien prophecy is an extreme example of dissonance. This conflict in beliefs versus truth can show up in countless places, including inaccurate answers to survey questions.

While adult entertainment is gaining some acceptance in our society, it's rare to hear someone proudly proclaim that he likes to visit porn sites on the Internet. In fact it's fair to say that the majority of porn consumers think of adult content as being unseemly and perhaps even perverse, yet they continue to visit sites, as evidenced by the billions of dollars that change hands in the industry every year.

If we go back to the hypothetical survey, perhaps the question of visiting adult sites is buried in the middle of the phone survey. When the question is asked, 'Do you visit adult sites online?', cognitive dissonance would cause some interviewees to quickly rationalize the gap between the truth (they do visit these sites) and the dissonant thought that this activity is in some ways unseemly. The answer then, to save face and resolve the conflict, is usually far from the truth, something like, 'No, I don't visit adult sites online.'

If we can't find an accurate number through vendors and we can't trust the response from consumers, then how are we going to estimate the size of the adult industry, or online gambling, or any other dissonance-causing issue that presents itself?

The answer lies in what I do for a living, looking at the anonymized and aggregate user behaviours for millions of US Internet users.

By observing our collective visits to adult websites, we're able to capture sizing data on the online adult industry in relation to the rest of the Web. Just how much of our online time is spent visiting adult sites, and how does demographic and search data give us more insight into what drives our online prurient interests? Since this data was so elusive using traditional market research, I became fascinated with the topic.

Given the low cost of entry, there are more than 40,000 adult sites in our database. That's more than twice the number of all online retail sites that we track. One of the things that stands out about the distribution of porn sites is just how fractionalized the spread is. The top 500 sites account for only 56 per cent of all visits to the adult category. (In contrast, the top 500 retail sites account for 76 per cent of all retail visits.) No doubt driven by the proliferation of online video, the amount of time spent on adult sites is on the increase. On average, as of August 2007, Internet users spent six minutes and twenty-nine seconds on any adult site within the category, up 15 per cent from two years prior, when average time on a porn site was five minutes and thirty-eight seconds.

When taken together, those 40,000 sites accounted for 10 per cent of all Internet visits in August 2007, down from 16 per cent in August 2005.

DAILY HABITS

While visits to adult sites may be falling at a precipitous rate, one pattern has held true over the last several years: the days of the week that we are more likely to visit adult sites. By breaking visit data down to daily increments, we find that Friday (most likely Friday evening) is consistently the weekly peak, followed closely by Saturday.

Throughout the year, the day with the least visits is Thanksgiving Day, perhaps due to the number of family members present in the household. Porn visits during the other weekdays tend to remain constant at 6 per cent below the Friday peak. Perhaps the Anglo-Christian tradition of Sunday as the Sabbath or seventh day, the day we should rest, is the reason that of all the days of the week, Sunday is on average the day with the least number of porn visits.

This probably comes as a pleasant surprise to Mike Foster and Craig Gross, who annually celebrate Porn Sunday on the first Sunday in October, a tradition that they started in 2005.

Gross founded xxxchurch.com, which he dubbed the '#1 Christian porn site' (the site is an anti-porn site). Touring the country in a tricked-out Scion xB, Gross's ministry is a non-denominational religious group focused on eliminating porn addiction. According to Matt Gross, God visited him one morning in the shower and had one word for him: 'pornography'. This 'in-shower' calling led Gross on his mission, which includes attending adult entertainment trade shows so he can hand out Bibles emblazoned with 'Jesus Loves Porn Stars.'[4]

Based on the theory that Internet users would be most likely to view adult content on the days that they're at home and have free time, we would expect that the weekend days, both Saturday and Sunday, would have the highest frequency of adult visits. Despite the fall in church attendance, and the decline in the percentage of the US population that identifies itself as religious, the fact that Sunday registers the lowest percentage of Internet visits confirms another theory: In the United States there is still some

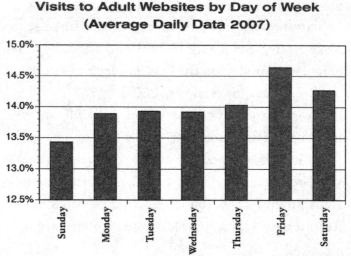

Visits to Adult Websites by Day of Week (Average Daily Data 2007)

Source: Hitwise

connection between our religious beliefs, Sundays, and the taboo nature of indulging. One possible hypothesis to explain the drop in adult Web visits on Sunday is that society has become more religious over time; but while our religious roots may explain why Sunday is the lightest porn day of the week, there is little to no evidence suggesting that our religious beliefs are affecting the overall use of online porn.

SOLVING THE 'WHO' OF adult content connoisseurs is a difficult job given the ubiquitous nature (excluding of course the dominance of male versus female visitors) of porn consumption. For the 40,634 adult sites tracked by Hitwise, on average 72.6 per cent of visitors were male and 27.4 per cent female. If you were expecting visitors to adult sites to be almost exclusively male, you were probably considering pornographic content in the form of pictures and videos. However, if you expand your focus to erotic literature, female preference for the written form of adult content becomes clear. For example, the site Adult-FanFiction.net, the largest of its kind, is predominantly visited by females (65.5 per cent), and, as we'll see, its audience is also young, 18–24 (54.6 per cent), something that is becoming increasingly atypical in the category.

The term 'fan fiction' refers to what was formerly an underground movement that can be traced to a time well before the Internet, to works of fiction created by fans of other works such as television sitcoms, movies and, in this case, erotica. The fan fiction movement dates back to mimeographed fan magazines like those for the fans of *Star Trek*. Today, many fan fiction sites flourish in a user-generated format where site visitors read or create fiction based on existing published adult novels, short stories and characters.

The other noteworthy trend in adult sites visited by women is on the business end of adult entertainment. In what was previously an industry dominated by male producers, directors and purveyors, the demographics of porn business sites, or those sites providing adult website hosting, marketing and transactional services, now reveal the increasing involvement of women.

Prior to the boom in home-based adult businesses, an adult movie required a film crew, capital investment in reproducing the film, and the wherewithal to distribute it to adult cinemas and bookshops. With the advent of the webcam and one-stop domain registration, hosting and payment solutions, for as little as a $100 capital investment in a webcam (assuming the aspiring adult star has a computer and high-speed

Internet connection) and $19.95 per month for domain hosting and shopping cart features, a new adult entrepreneur can be in business.

A REGIONAL BREAKDOWN OF adult content visitors reveals only a slight skew to some states, with the Midwest Internet user slightly more likely to visit adult sites than users in the rest of the country. The states with users least likely to visit adult sites are the newest states in the union, Hawaii and Alaska. This pattern can change depending on the time of year, particularly during winter, when there is a marked increase in porn activity for cold-weather states.

Visits to Adult Websites, Top 10 States by Index

State	Representation against the Online Population	Traffic Share
Ohio	124.03	5.87%
Minnesota	121.74	2.51%
Wisconsin	120.61	2.38%
Iowa	117.22	1.00%
New Hampshire	117.12	0.61%
Colorado	115.00	2.19%
Massachusetts	114.56	2.90%
Indiana	114.37	2.53%
Kansas	113.96	0.79%
West Virginia	112.00	0.52%

Source: Hitwise

If we break Internet visitors by state into their
Republican-state and Democrat-state contingents
and then rank adult sites by their percentage of contribution to overall use in those states, we find that
Republican-state visitors are likely to visit
wife-swapping sites, adult webcams, adult match-
making services, and sites devoted to voyeurism,
while Democrat-state visitors are most likely to visit
directories for adult entertainers and escorts.

UNDERSTANDING THE
DECLINE IN ADULT VISITS

When we compare visits to the category of Social
Networks and Forums (where all social networks,
such as MySpace and Facebook, are categorized) to
visits to the Adult category, the pattern appears to
show a negative correlation. Could social networking activity be a substitute for visits to adult sites?

While anecdotal, two days in the summer of 2006
may hold some insight into the trade-off between
social networking and porn.

On 22 July 2006, a very warm day in Southern
California, something went very wrong at 1200 West
Seventh Street in Los Angeles, also known as the Gar-
land Building. The building housed the servers for
MySpace. The home page for the most popular do-
main name on the Internet, which at the time ac-

Market Share of Visits to Adult and Social Network Sites

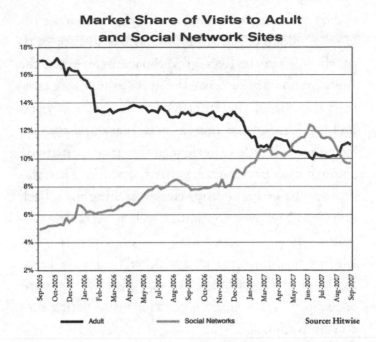

Source: Hitwise

counted for 4 per cent of all Internet visits in the United States – more than 17 per cent of all pages viewed – displayed a short, casual message from founder Tom Anderson saying, 'Hey everyone! There's been a power outage in our data center. We're in the process of fixing it right now, so sit tight. – Tom'

As a result of the outage, a curious thing began to happen: As news of the outage spread, visits to MySpace increased significantly. One explanation could be that users, exhibiting signs of social network addiction, were visiting the site repeatedly in the hope that the outage had been resolved.

For me as a researcher, the MySpace outage offered a unique opportunity. What would happen to fill the void in the lives of MySpace users when the site went down? For those two days in July we examined the rest of the Internet by site and category, looking for unusual increases in market share. We found that Google experienced the greatest increase compared to previous days of the week. This was most probably caused by users searching for a back door into MySpace content as well as searching recreationally . . . If I can't hang out on MySpace, then I'll just randomly search for other things to do on the Internet. There were two categories that experienced increases during the outage: online dating sites and adult sites.

Another possible explanation for the drop in market share for the adult category lies in the changes in age demographic over time. The percentage of 18–24-year-olds who visit the adult category has dropped from 15.9 per cent at the end of 2006 to 13.4 per cent for the same time period in 2007. The same is true for the 25–34-year-old age group, which has dropped from 24.1 per cent to 18.6 per cent. These are the two groups that have also seen dramatic increases in visits to social networking websites. Taking all of this data together appears to indicate that there is indeed a trade-off between the two types of sites. Search-term patterns, more specifically the search for sex, further confirm this theory.

'Sex' is one of the most popular searches on the Internet, in the number 120 position among all search terms in summer 2007. A Google search on the term results in 445 million entries returned in .07 seconds. Sex searches also display an interesting pattern, with the queries increasing in the summer months and an unexplained spike each year the week of Christmas. (This is one of the search phenomena that have been in my unsolved mysteries folder for quite some time. One possible explanation is that visits to porn sites spike when we have more time on our hands.) If we look back two years, when social networking sites were much smaller than they are today, searches for 'sex' went to a variety of sites, including sites dedicated to sex education (www. sexetc.org) and articles about sex (www.salon.com). If we fast-forward to the summer of 2007, that same search term drove traffic to online video sites (www.metacafe.com and video.google.com), a social encyclopedia (www.wikipedia.org) and social network MySpace, indicating that consumption of online adult content has moved from the world of static display of images and video to the world of Web 2.0, where consumer-generated media and social networks now play a key role.

In November 2007 I wrote on the subject of social networks versus porn in my weekly online Science of Search column for *TIME*. At that point I had acquired more than 900 new Facebook 'friends' through a similar column on that social network the week before. Several college students (all, I'm assuming, in the 18–24 demographic) sent me messages through Facebook to comment on my story. The theme running through all messages on the subject was that social networks were replacing visits to adult sites because those networks have given young users the ability to connect with other singles in an unprecedented way. To quote one of my newfound young friends, 'Who needs porn when Facebook gives you the opportunity to hook up in the flesh?' He may have a point. In fact, visits to the online dating category have been on a steady decline as well, with the younger generation by 2003–2004 using first-generation social networks such as Friendster as a competitive substitute for dating sites.

Online behavioural data is shedding new light on topics that aren't readily accessible by traditional research methods. This new view has applications beyond the adult industry. Take gambling, for example.

* * *

IN THE AUTUMN OF 2005 I found myself in the basement of the Excalibur Hotel in Las Vegas, wondering to myself, What am I doing here? I speak regularly around the country at technology and travel conferences, leading universities – how did I end up here? This was my first online gambling conference. As I entered the exhibition hall I was greeted by a woman with a strong cockney accent. ''Allo, love,' she said. I took the opportunity to inquire a little bit about the audience for this event. 'Isn't online gambling illegal in the US, and if so, isn't it risky for businesses that work in this industry to gather in a public place?' My new friend leaned in a little with a sly smile and said, 'The ones at risk here travel under an alias.'

To this day I don't know if she was just pulling my leg, but I took her reply to be the truth as I headed towards the auditorium to take my place on-stage. I was there to present the concept of online competitive intelligence to this group of online poker, blackjack and casino game sites. My MO at trade conferences is to pick a random company from the attendee list and present slides showing exactly what I could discern about their specific site: where they receive their traffic from (search engines, email campaigns, affiliates), where they rank in relation to their competitors in visits, even the search terms that they're purchasing to get traffic to the site. It didn't dawn on me until mid-speech that it probably wasn't a good idea to pick on anyone in this crowd. (Scenes from *The Sopranos* played in my head.)

I decided to wrap things up quickly and get out of the room as swiftly as possible. Just before I made the exit, a gentleman running a poker site from Costa Rica stopped me in my path. 'This data's amazing,' he said. 'I've always believed that there was a trade-off between online sports betting and poker, but I've never seen the data to prove it.' He was speaking about one of my slides, which used search behaviour to show that betting budgets were a zero-sum game. I had to stick around to explain this one.

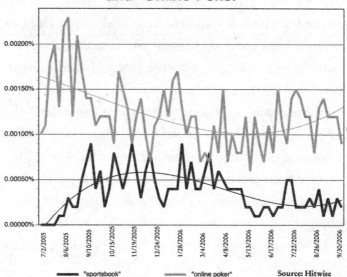

Volume of Searches on "Sportsbook" and "Online Poker"

Within my research group we had noticed a pattern between searches for 'online poker' and 'sportsbook' over time. It appeared as though the two terms were negatively correlated, or in other words, when 'online poker' searches increased, searches for 'sportsbook' decreased, and vice versa. Before drawing the chart, we had a theory that online gamblers had a limited budget with which they wagered on the Internet. Since online poker is a year-round non-seasonal activity, if there was no interdependence between the two gambling activities there should be no trade-off in traffic.

The chart, however, revealed that as 'sportsbook' activity reaches its peak during football and basketball seasons, 'online poker' action decreases. This is most probably explained as a trade-off: If there are no sports bets for me to place, I'll gamble on online poker instead of waiting for the next sports season. My friend from Costa Rica had had trouble figuring out the seasonal swings of poker traffic. This chart offered a new explanation that made total sense.

In the realm of vice categories of traffic, online gambling is small compared to porn. If you were to group all gambling sites (including sites that provide lottery information for all fifty states), visits to those sites would equal one-eighteenth of the adult category total.

Just as you might gather from walking around a casino floor in Las Vegas, Atlantic City or Reno, the people most willing to wager online are not necessarily the ones who can afford it. Out of all visitors to the Gambling category, 24.7 per cent had household incomes of less than $30,000 per year, and 53.5 per cent of visitors earned $60,000 or less per year. And, perhaps the reason that the high limits sections in casinos are so small, only 7 per cent of online gambling visitors were in the highest income bracket that we measured, those earning more than $150,000 per year.

Examining the difference between online poker players and sports betters (during the peak sports periods and the off periods) helps identify the swing better who trades off for poker during the off-season, as opposed to the diehard poker player. When you compare sports betters and poker players online, poker players are found to have the strongest representation in the $60,000–$100,000 bracket, while the one income segment that swings towards poker only during the off-season is the lower income segment of $30,000–$60,000, which demonstrates that on the Internet gambling activities can differ by socio-economic status. As we will find through subsequent chapters, there are clear differences in how people of different ages, income levels and geographic regions use the Internet. Yet there are other examples that transcend all demographic boundaries. Take the magic little blue pill, for example.

SOME INDUSTRY FIGURES PLACE the proliferation of spam email at more than 80 per cent of messages in our inboxes. It seems as though those generating spam are outsmarting ISPs and the spam-filtering software that tries to distinguish relevant messages that are important to our lives from unsolicited advertisements for everything from get-rich-quick schemes, Nigerian bank scams and weight-loss remedies to various devices that promise to enlarge our private appendages and above all provide low-cost solutions for erectile dysfunction. More than 20 per cent of all inbox spam is in some way related to Viagra. But why? Are these promulgators of endless email messages actually hoping that we will click through and purchase an offshore pharmaceutical?

For Viagra spammers it's a numbers game, sometimes with click-through rates (CTRs) as low as in the hundredths of a per cent. Spammers quickly learned that if you send out enough emails there is profit to be made. One Australian spammer was accused of sending out more than 2 billion Viagra spam emails in the course of a year.

Spammers have become increasingly resourceful in finding ways to send millions of emails per day and avoid detection. While the early Internet spammer might have used a single server to send out spam, that method was too easily traceable. 'Instead, sophisticated spammers use parasitic software programs known as Trojan horses to hijack individual computers and use them as remote servers for sending spam. The method is virtually impossible to prosecute because spammers can take over an unsuspecting user's computer, send millions of emails in a few hours, and leave without a trace.'[5]

So what are the economics behind all these emails? Take a US prescription for Viagra. It's likely to cost around $10.00 to $15.00 per tablet. However, in countries where the patent on sildenafil citrate has expired, or where there is little or no regulation on the production of pharmaceuticals, the same drug can be produced for less than $2.00 a pill. The Internet has solved a problem faced by the producers of low-cost knock-off drugs: how to sell and distribute these pharmaceuticals. Direct-to-consumer (DTC) advertising is heavily regulated in the United States, often making marketing a costly proposition. But overseas producers use affiliate relationships to lessen their costs.

In a model pioneered in the mid-nineties with Amazon.com, affiliate partners provide the perfect sales channel for this business. Amazon, in an effort to expand its sales power, offered any person with a website the ability to add links for books available on the Amazon site. Any books sold from traffic sent by an affiliate would result in an affiliate fee paid back to the owner of that website. The affiliate earned anywhere from 4 to 10 per cent of the resulting sale.

Producers of overseas sildenafil citrate, interested in selling as many pills as possible without being responsible for violating local laws, leveraged this model to recruit affiliates, which could be anyone with the ability to generate orders for a fee as much as 40 per cent per transaction.

The overwhelming volume of Viagra spam and other unsolicited emails is sent at an estimated rate of 12.4 billion messages per day. Some estimate that 8 per cent of US Internet users who have received this spam have purchased products from those emails.

The deluge of Viagra messages in our inboxes may partly explain the popularity of the drug online. Over the course of the last two years, spikes in searches on 'Viagra' have been concurrent with massive Viagra spam blasts. As of autumn 2007, Viagra was the third most searched-for drug, behind weight-loss drug alli and depression anxiety drug Lexapro.

Searches for erectile dysfunction drugs served as one of the first examples we found of seasonal trends in the way we search for things on the Internet. In the case of drugs such as Viagra, Levitra and Cialis, things come to a head in late January and early February, right around the Super Bowl. Over the last four years, since starting at Hitwise, I have had a Super Bowl tradition that includes a high-definition television, a barbecue, a few beers and a spreadsheet. Each year I study the effects of Super Bowl commercials on Web traffic and, more recently, on search patterns. As with the spike on erectile dysfunction searches, each year the data shows that repeated spots can drive us to find out more information online.

Not all seasonal Internet behavioural patterns are driven by television commercials; some are just ingrained in our society. Internet behaviour can reveal a great deal about society. Some of the most interesting patterns are those that surround our visits and searches in the realm of politics. From a market research perspective, estimating our political convictions has proven to be a very difficult and often elusive challenge. Online behaviour provides a fresh perspective.

CHAPTER **2**

Getting to What We Really Think

What do we really mean? It's a question that keeps market researchers up at night. Discerning what a large group of the population is thinking at any given time is actually much more difficult than just asking them what they're thinking. One of the first challenges in getting the answers right is to make sure that you're posing the question to the right cross-section of people. If you've wondered why pre-election polls seem increasingly less accurate, this could be one of the key reasons.

There's some history to this dilemma. In fact, according to the *Literary Digest* poll of 1936, our thirty-second president shouldn't have been Franklin Roosevelt, but instead his Republican opponent, Alf Landon.

Roosevelt's landslide victory came as quite a shock to voters, who were expecting a landslide victory for Landon. After all, the magazine had correctly predicted the five previous presidential races. In retrospect, the majority of critics pointed to sampling error as the reason for the big disconnect between what the survey had predicted and the actual Election Day results. In the post-mortem analysis of what went wrong in calling Roosevelt versus Landon, you really didn't have to look much further than the selection bias behind who filled out the response card used to collect the results.

In fielding their straw poll, the digest used a unique sampling method. In order to mail out more than 10 million surveys, they relied on automobile registrations and telephone directories.[6] If you consider the year, 1936, you'll realize that only certain households were wealthy enough to afford a telephone or an automobile. Those wealthier individuals were also more likely to be Republicans supporting Landon.

In fact, one of the biggest challenges in market research is predicting how voters will cast their ballots when they've entered their local polling place and pulled the black curtain. Recent elections have revealed the inability of pre-election research to predict the final results. One potential reason for the difference between what the polls say and the reality of election results can be found in what we discussed in the previous chapter: People don't always accurately answer questions about their beliefs and future actions. From the way that we search online for information on candidates, it appears that the deciding factor for some voters isn't the political party or even the candidate's stance on specific issues. For a large portion of Internet-enabled voters, character, even appearance, can drive decisions. And though we may not want to admit it, things like religious affiliation can play a critical role.

On 19 January 2007, less than a month before his announcement that he would run for president, a news report appeared on Fox News saying that Barack Obama had attended an Islamic madrassa in his early childhood, from 1967 to 1971. The Fox News story was discredited in a CNN segment that aired four days later, on 23 January. The CNN reporter visiting the Basuki school, which Barack had attended in Indonesia, found no evidence that the school was teaching radical Islamic principles. Basuki was a public school that did not focus on religion.

While the madrassa rumour, at four days, was particularly short-lived, the emotionally charged connection of a presidential candidate to a school system with links to the Taliban clearly had an impact on the voting public. If we look at the way Internet users searched for information about Barack Obama prior to the story airing on Fox, we find that of the top 150 searches on the candidate most queries were looking for information about Obama's background and the speech that he gave at the Democratic Convention in 2004, with some queries about his religion.

Here are the top ten searches that contained 'Barack Obama' in the four weeks ending 30 December 2006:

1. Barack Obama
2. Barack Obama biography
3. 'Barack Obama'
4. Obama Barack
5. Barack Obama's religion
6. Senator Barack Obama
7. Barack Obama speech
8. Barack Obama religion
9. Barack Obama the Audacity of Hope
10. Barack Obama Muslim

Immediately after the madrassa story broke on Fox, the searches around Obama shifted dramatically. The search for 'Barack Obama Muslim' moved from being the tenth to being the fifth most popular query containing the candidate's name. Searches that contained 'Barack Obama' also doubled when compared to the week before the story.

Following the madrassa rumour, there was a marked increase in searches for Obama's religious views, specifically his association with Islam. Viewed from a different perspective: Of all of the searches containing the word 'Muslim' in the week following the Fox News story, three of the top ten searches contained some reference to Barack Obama.

One of the most remarkable aspects of the Barack Obama madrassa misinformation incident is the half-life of associations created by a story that had only four days before it was discounted. If we look at search behaviour one year later, three of the top ten search terms that contain 'Barack Obama' reference his religion or the Muslim religion, and if we look at the searches that contain 'Muslim', six of the top ten terms contain a mention of Barack Obama.

While political research using the aggregate behaviour of Internet users does pose challenges – the biggest being that you can't pose specific questions – one of the advantages is that often actions speak louder than words. Another advantage is that you don't have to worry about the issues of cognitive dissonance discussed in Chapter 1. While an individual might fear being labelled a racist if he or she admitted in a survey to being so concerned about a candidate's attendance at a Muslim elementary school, that same concern would be clearly visible in the individual's search terms.

Gleaning insight from search-term data as we've done in politics also has distinct advantages in other areas, such as brand marketing, in which a brand's strength can be measured by how often and in what ways Internet users search for it.

THIS EXERCISE OF MEASURING the strength and associations of a positive or negative event involving a brand has some obvious business implications. One of the advantages of using observed Internet data to measure brand strength is the timeliness of the feedback.

When I arrived at the Columbia Business School to appear on a panel at the Innovative Marketing Summit, I was a little early, so I decided to sit in the audience and listen to some of the other presenters. Onstage that morning was Deepak Advani, the chief marketing officer of Lenovo.

Lenovo, a Beijing-based computer company founded in the mid-1980s, purchased the personal computer division of IBM in 2005 for $1.27 billion. At the time there was some scepticism of Lenovo's ability to continue building the ThinkPad brand that had such close associations with its former parent IBM.

Deepak was giving a fascinating talk about his company's purchase of ThinkPad. After providing some examples of the way that his marketing department was influencing the perception of the Think-Pad and Lenovo brands, he began to field questions from the audience. One conference attendee asked a very basic question: How effective was all the effort Deepak had put into boosting the brand? Deepak answered that they were fielding brand studies and he planned to have some results several months later.

With the pervasiveness of wireless hot spots and laptops that have built-in wireless capability, conference audiences have turned keynotes into multitasking events, half-listening to presentations while simultaneously answering email and browsing the Web. As a speaker, I've always felt a little put off by the half-listening conference-goer. Applying the Golden Rule to the situation, I make it a habit to give other speakers my undivided attention. But in this case, I just couldn't resist. Deepak didn't have to wait several months for results; I could get some quick initial feedback on the effectiveness of his campaigns within one to two minutes.

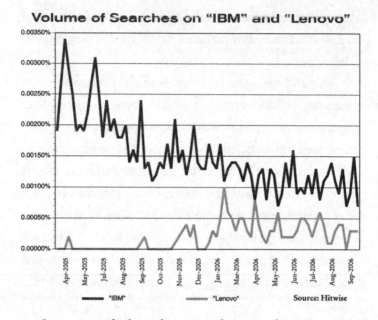

Volume of Searches on "IBM" and "Lenovo"

Sure enough, based on search-term share it would seem that with the handover of the ThinkPad brand IBM began losing brand equity, while Lenovo simultaneously gained ground to almost reach parity with IBM by the week before the conference.

Longing for a true Web 2.0 experience, I looked at my watch and calculated that I had ten minutes before my talk started. Plenty of time to publish this chart and some analysis on my blog before I had to speak. I checked search-term suggestions and found the associations for the Lenovo brand, such as 'new think pad', 'Lenovo think pad', and 'Lenovo laptop'. There were searches for the T60 model and concerns over battery life, as well as interest in where a potential purchaser could see a demonstration model to help make a decision to buy.

When I took the stage to talk about the use of Internet data to help make business decisions, I directed everyone to my blog. I was showboating at this point to demonstrate that in the last fifteen minutes I was able to come up with an answer to a question from another speaker that would have been several months in coming by way of traditional survey-based brand studies.

Search and Internet behavioural data can go beyond simply providing the strength of a candidate or a computer's brand; it can provide insight into the decision process itself, and unlike with traditional surveys, this observed behaviour isn't skewed by any participant selection bias.

IN THE WORLD OF online politics, the brand insight we gained from the Obama madrassa story led us down another path. When a voter decides what candidate to vote for in an election, what is his or her decision based on? The candidate's political record or stance on key issues, or is it just a gut feeling based on background or even looks?

There are growing problems with political polling, some legislative and some reflected in how choices in telecommunications are affecting the reliability of all random-digit dial-phone surveys.

In 2003 Congress enacted the Do-Not-Call Implementation Act, which, in a programme instigated by the Federal Trade Commission, allowed individuals to place their home phone on a list if they didn't want to be contacted by telemarketers. Consumers rejoiced in the prospect of eating their dinner in peace and quiet without having to answer a sales call regarding the new time-share deal of a lifetime. But it appeared that market researchers had little to worry about, since there were exceptions for market research calls as well as calls from charitable organizations and political parties.

Regardless of the exception, the job of the telephone surveyor has become increasingly difficult since 2003 because, even though the Do-Not-Call Registry doesn't apply to market research, it had the effect of empowering consumers to 'just say no' to any unsolicited phone calls that were interrupting their increasingly busy days.

Even more surprising is that the issues that the *Literary Digest* faced in the infamous pre-election poll of 1936 may be resurfacing. In a recent study, the Centers for Disease Control looked at the number of households that have abandoned their corded landline phones, instead deciding to use their mobile phones as their primary residential phone. This issue is of great importance to the CDC, as a random-digital dial survey is the primary method that the agency uses to track national health conditions and risk behaviour. If the sample of respondents doesn't represent the overall US population, the results are not as trustworthy. Cord-cutters, a label that research firm In-Stat had adopted to describe these mobile-phone-only homes, are increasing at a growing rate. More troubling for surveyors and pollsters is that 22 per cent of poorer households are cord-cutters, nearly double the number of more affluent households. Why is this important?

Pre-election polls, like those that missed their predictions in the 2008 primaries, are random-digit dial-telephone surveys that traditionally call only landline phones, much in the way that *Literary Digest*'s poll reached only households that could afford a telephone. In today's world, landline-only polls undercount the poor as well as younger voters, forcing many pollsters to consider including a more costly mobile phone sample in their future polls.

While recent studies indicate that the exclusion of mobile-phone-only households has a minimal impact on poll results, significant increases in the numbers of these mobile-phone-only individuals and rapidly decreasing participation rates for both mobile and landline participants will increase the difficulty of contacting a truly representative sample.

If we look at the top candidates vying for their party's nomination in the 2008 presidential race, we find that, as with Obama, searches for candidates may not reveal interest in political views, but often focus on elements of a candidate's personal life that arguably have little bearing on his or her ability to lead the country. For Republican front-runner John McCain, for example, in January 2008 top searches focused on information about his wife, family and daughter in that order. Internet searchers looking for information on Hillary Clinton in the same time period were looking for jokes, cartoons and information about her crying prior to the New Hampshire primary.

Interestingly, the long-shot Republican candidate after Super Tuesday, Mike Huckabee, who was known in the press as the evangelical candidate, given his prior vocation as a pastor, unlike Barack Obama had no mention of his religion in the top searches on his name. Rather, searchers were interested in his association with Chuck Norris, who in endorsing Huckabee was seen onstage with him at several public events.

Search data appears to tell us that Internet searchers are more interested in the image of the candidate than they are in the candidate's stance on issues or his or her voting record. But it would be unfair to extrapolate from that that as a country we're not interested in political issues. Rather, we just don't spend much time associating candidates with those issues, at least not on the Internet.

Online politics is a relatively small fraction of our Internet surfing behaviour. The 756 sites that comprise the Hitwise Politics category accounted for only 0.23 per cent of all Internet visits for the month of January 2008. To put that in perspective, categories such as fashion, insurance, lotteries and gambling all had more traffic than the Politics category.

Still, when we examine search terms that are sending traffic to political sites, we find that there are several terms that give us insight into what the top political issues are for any given week. Amid searches for candidates, top political blogs and polling results are searches for the issues. Consistently, over the last several years, the number one political search term has been 'abortion', followed by 'death penalty' in a distant second and, for the month of January 2008, 'national debt', which is a newcomer to the issue list, most likely due to fear of a looming recession.

CONSIDERING SOME OF THE confounding variables that exist in the online politics category, you can see

why it is so hard to predict election outcomes based
on Internet behaviour and search behaviour specifically. Like the cross-over patterns in political surfing
that occur the closer we are to an election, other complications, such as demographics and the online savvy
of a specific candidate's supporters, can make predictions even more troublesome. There is no better example of this complication than the Ron Paul effect.

When the Texas congressman began his campaign
for the White House, he raised more than a few eye-
brows. While running for the Republican nomination, Ron Paul espoused a policy that was decidedly
libertarian: minimize government, including elimi-
nation of the Internal Revenue Service and other federal agencies. In the pre-election polls before the
primaries, Ron Paul's support hovered in the low
single digits, registering between 2 and 4 per cent of
Republican voters. The odd thing was that his Internet numbers were off the chart. Heading into Super
Tuesday's primary, Ron Paul had the most visited
website of any political candidate, Democrat or Republican. He also had more searches than any other
candidate. Why then was Ron Paul so low in the actual polls and the resulting primary vote?

The seemingly aberrant gap between Paul's popular vote and our Internet data was not specific to
Hitwise. Ron Paul's dominance was appearing

throughout several measurement services, including Google Trends, a service from Google that
ranks the overall search volume of specific terms.
On 9 October CNBC hosted an online poll asking
readers to vote for their favourite candidate in the
Michigan Republican debates. The votes for Ron
Paul were overwhelming, registering more than 75
per cent. The results were so dramatic that Allen
Wastler, managing editor of CNBC.com, posted an
open letter to 'the Ron Paul Faithful' explaining
that the results of the CNBC.com poll, giving Paul
the landslide victory in the debate, were so far from
any other 'legit' poll that he had decided to take the
poll down for fear that it had been hacked or was
the subject of a campaign to deliberately inflate
Paul's numbers. But who exactly were those users
searching for Ron Paul?

The largest segment of visitors to Ron Paul's site
was the Young Digerati, described by the Southern
California company Claritas this way: 'Affluent,
highly educated, and ethnically mixed, Young Digerati communities are typically filled with trendy
apartments and condos, fitness clubs and clothing
boutiques, casual restaurants and all types of bars –
from juice to coffee to microbrew.' Of the sixty-six
segments that made up the visitors to the Ron Paul
site, Young Digerati accounted for 15.4 per cent.

We'll learn more about Young Digerati and other Early Adopters in Chapter 10.

The technical prowess of this specific group might help explain the gap between online and traditional polls. To address Wastler's point: If any group had the technical wherewithal to mount a campaign to win an online poll, this was the group. And on the other hand, the characteristics of the Young Digerati might make this group skew towards another characteristic: cord-cutting.

There was arguably little hope that Ron Paul would win the Republican nomination for president in the 2008 elections, and the disconnection between what we observed online in terms of his popularity as measured by visits to his site, and what pre-election data told us, just continued to widen. But even though this specific candidate might not have had a chance in this election, the more troubling question is, as the percentage of cord-cutters among the population grows, how will the increasingly inaccurate traditional polls skew the actual voting activity of the American public? If polls do act as self-fulfilling prophecies (if my candidate has such little support in the polls, then why should I waste a vote on him/her?), inaccurate poll results could alter voter behaviour and ultimately final election results.

* * *

BLOG TRAFFIC GIVES US even more insight into the way we digest political information online. Matt Hindman, a political science professor at Arizona State University, had an idea of how we might apply our data to see how traffic flows through political blogs. While ranking views of sites by market share and clickstream reports (detailed inventories of where people come from and where they go to when they visit a particular site) is very useful in itself, Matt had the idea of combining the two data sources and mapping the politics category in a network map format.

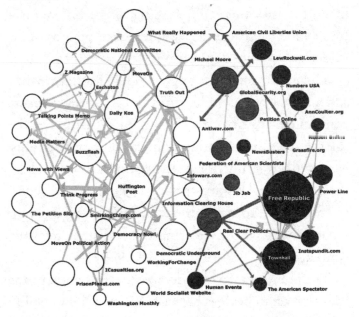

Source: Matt Hindman and Anthony Hayes

When we combine the elements of size and traffic source in a map of the online political landscape, we can see which sites act as hubs and which sites are on the periphery, and by colour-coding political sites by ideology (white for Democratic, black for Republican and grey for nonpartisan sites), we can see, among other things, the difference in how Democrats and Republicans surf.

The first difference that is clear from this snapshot taken in May 2007 is that traffic to right-leaning blogs tends to be much more insular in nature. If you visit Townhall.com or Ann Coulter.com, you are less likely to visit other right-leaning blogs, unlike visitors to their left-leaning counterparts, who create a spider web of interconnections.

There are sites among the left-leaning white spheres that act as hubs, sites like Huffingtonpost.com and DailyKos.com, which find themselves in the middle of left-leaning political blog traffic. This is most likely a function of their popularity as well as their generous linking policy, which freely sends traffic off-site to read other articles, as well as lures readers back with a clearing-house list of relevant content.

The political map also demonstrates that there are sites that act as bridges between left and right ideologies. Sites like Real Clear Politics and FreeRepublic.

com stand out as virtual bridges between the two groups of political thought.

But Hindman's map is just a snapshot. From the presidential election in 2004 we know that traffic patterns around political sites, as well as search terms on top candidates, can become very muddled, which is one of the reasons that it becomes nearly impossible to gauge popularity and ultimately predict election results based solely on website visits and search-term volume. What we observed leading up to the 2004 election was that the closer we came to primaries and elections, the more 'cross-over' behaviour became apparent in the data set. This is most

Political Websites Visited Immediately After Visits to FoxNews.com (February 2008)

Site	Downstream Share
You Decide 2008	9.20%
Real Clear Politics	0.33%
Major Garrett's Bourbon Room	0.13%
Michael Savage	0.11%
Mike Huckabee	0.09%
Power Line	0.09%
Fred '08	0.06%
The Politico	0.05%
Human Events Online	0.05%
NewsBusters	0.05%

Source: Hitwise

likely explained by people's desire to solidify their decision on candidates based on opposing viewpoints, as well as their interest in finding the weaknesses in opposing ideologies.

An interesting corollary to this concept of measuring political thought processes through clickstream data is the use of this same data to understand political bias in traditional news coverage (or bias in news coverage audiences). If, for example, I were to look at the political websites visited just prior to and just after users visited the FoxNews.com website, the list of sites would be dominated by right-leaning blogs and personalities.

If, instead, I draw up the same list for CBSNews.com, with the exception of visits going to and from Mike Huckabee's website (due to his primary wins in January and February 2008), the majority of sites lean to the left, such as DailyKos and Huffingtonpost.

While the clickstream habits of news sites may not be proof of coverage bias, at a minimum they show that a certain audience, with a defined viewpoint, is attracted to a news website. This same type of analysis can be applied to newspaper sites, even to official candidate websites, to help determine what the political leanings are for visitors to that site.

Clickstream data, or information on sites visited

immediately before and after any given site or category of site, can also provide new insight to businesses. If we consider how tracking users as they jump from site to site can be applied to news and entertainment content on the Web, we see that we have a new way of viewing competitive space. For example, ask the publishers of any magazine which other magazines they consider among their competitors, and I can almost guarantee that magazine websites visited before and after their own will contain titles they have never considered competitive before.

I was visiting a publisher client in New York last year and the topic of competitive magazines came

Political Websites Visited Immediately After Visits to CBSNews.com (February 2008)

Site	Downstream Share
CBSNews – Elections	1.50%
Real Clear Politics	0.46%
The Huffington Post	0.24%
The Politico	0.16%
ICasualties	0.14%
Talking Points Memo	0.09%
MyDD Direct Democracy	0.08%
Daily Kos	0.08%
You Decide 2008	0.06%
Human Events Online	0.06%

Source: Hitwise

up. My client (who manages titles that range from fashion to news to other topics) was focusing on one of her leading titles in the fashion industry. Of course the editors at this magazine considered all of the other leading women's fashion magazines their competitors. But by examining clickstream data I could provide a view, on a national scale, of what online magazine readers pick up from the virtual magazine rack just before and after viewing my client's title.

As it turned out, the other women's fashion magazines were indeed in the clickstream of my client's title, but they were secondary to another group of fashion magazine sites, those for teen fashion.[7] The editors scoffed at my finding – it didn't make sense; their brand was clearly much more upmarket. But it's hard to dispute the hard data that online consumer behaviour provides. By analysing the demographics and psychographics of visitors to my client's site, we discovered that a specific group of teens, those living in upscale urban and suburban households, had a cross-over behaviour not exhibited by other groups. In fact, these upscale teens were exhibiting interest in fashion titles that their more rural counterparts were not.

As in politics, in fashion and in other categories – retail, pharmaceuticals, travel – a wealth of knowledge can be obtained about who consumers actually are (often different from who we think they are), which sheds new light on which consumers businesses in these categories should be marketing towards.

While market research techniques have come a long way since the *Literary Digest* poll of 1936, more than seventy years later we still face the persistent problem of finding a representative sample for accurate results. A large sample of Internet users constructed to accurately reflect the population (or at least the online population) goes a long way towards providing additional insight. Internet data also goes a lot further, in supplying us with insights that weren't available in the past. Those insights, however, are not always as easy to come by as the analysis of a straightforward survey question.

By the end of 2008 you might guess that the story of the year was the election of Barack Obama as the United State's 44th president and the first African American to hold that position. Media coverage of the election would confirm your hunch. Search data, however, paints a different picture. The collective search patterns of American Internet users reveals that the campaign celebrity with the greatest spike in searches wasn't Obama or McCain, but the Republican vice-presidential candidate, Alaska Governor Sarah Palin.

When I initially charted the massive spike in Palin searches, I hypothesized that the volume of searches on the candidate must be related to the fact that few

Americans had any knowledge of the Alaskan Governor. A quick look at the search terms containing her name revealed that Internet users were not looking for her biography or voting record; the most common category of searches was for pictures of Sarah Palin, or more specifically 'hot pictures of Sarah Palin'.

On further investigation this superficial fascination with candidate celebrity wasn't limited to Palin; in fact one of the most popular searches for McCain wasn't for the Republican presidential candidate but rather for his daughter Meghan and speculation around her lunch with reality television star Heidi Montag. Even Obama queries focused on seemingly irrelevant factoids such as 'how tall is Barack Obama?'.

What was missing from candidate searches was searches for the candidate's stances on issues and voting record. Those queries did eventually surface in the top of the political search term lists, but not until the week before the election.

Mining through observed behaviour, at times, is like a treasure hunt. It requires both the right-brain skill of seeing patterns in the data and the left-brain ability to formulate a hypothesis and then test it with the data at hand. Take prom dresses, for example . . .

CHAPTER 3

Prom in January

Timing is everything – from swinging a bat at just the right moment to send a ball over the fence, to timing the delivery of a joke to elicit the maximum amount of laughter. Some believe that timing is an innate skill, but as Internet data reveals, sometimes our skill at understanding when things become important to us can be a little off. In a world where our interest in topics is cyclical, a repeating pattern, do we really know when peaks and troughs actually occur?

Take, for example, the optimum time that a clothing retailer decides to feature prom dresses online. If you are like the majority of retailers, you would reason that with most school proms occurring in May, March to April would be the optimum time to put prom dress content online. Unfortunately, if you followed that reasoning, you would miss the biggest opportunity to capitalize on the flood of prom dress interest that occurs every year.

If we can't trust our gut instinct on timing, like a major-league baseball hitter or headlining stand-up comic, how can we find the right moment? That's where Internet data comes in.

Through the noise, as an Internet researcher, I began to realize that the interesting by-product of the social-networking and consumer-generated media revolution is that, as the Internet moves from a vast group of static pages we did little but read to an environment where users are posting volumes of data about their personal lives, I have an ever-growing, rich database from which to understand our society, or, more specifically, what people are thinking about collectively at any given moment.

Where others might find useless ramblings, I find colour to inform some of the patterns that I see in the data. That's where online personas come into play. I decided to spend a few hours in MySpace to help understand the patterns that I saw around prom dress searches. There's no shortage of prom dress obsession in MySpace profiles, so I found what I was looking for. Let's call the first persona I put together 'Taylor'.

From reading profiles of the younger generation, I can first see how communication patterns have changed since my school days. Email, for example, is so last year. With Facebook and MySpace, my invented subject is a few clicks away from discovering what all of her friends are up to – where they are, what they are listening to and watching. Taylor is a member of a new generation, characterized as 'Generation Next', living a life of connectedness that I can barely fathom as a forty-year-old analyst covering the Internet industry. In my teens I was reachable by a knock on the front door or a call to my parents' corded phone. For the majority of the day, if in school, at the dinner table or after 10 pm, I was completely disconnected from my friends. Taylor's connectedness is much more complete, through sites like Twitter, where she can post snippets of her thoughts for the entire Web to see. When she actively posts, we essentially have a portal into her consciousness. She is contactable online via email and instant message, and when on the go she can be reached via mobile phone, text messaging preferred.

Taylor lives a privileged life that revolves primarily around her friends and fashion, all of which she makes abundantly clear on her MySpace page. She's a varsity cheerleader, solid B student, and member of the school's French and 4-H clubs. Despite her extracurricular activities, Taylor's MySpace page reveals an obsession: her senior prom. In fact the entire left-hand side of her well-thought-out 'pro', or profile, is a rolling slideshow of pictures featuring her and her friends at their junior prom the previous year. Taylor's page is complete with an embedded MP3 file of Edwin McCain singing the theme from *A Cinderella Story*, 'I'll Be', one of the favourite slow songs from the junior prom.

By browsing through her page, and the seemingly endless forwarded questionnaires that she's filled out (Generation Next's answer to the chain letter), we learn, among other things, that she loves to watch *The OC*, *Laguna Beach*, *Real World*, *America's Top Model* and of course *American Idol*.

The top ten of Taylor's 461 online 'friends' are listed on her page as well. In today's age of texting, MySpace pages and that old standby, email, teens find themselves with a connection, albeit mostly electronic, to a vast social network that is far greater than in the pre-Internet days when I was in high school. The nature of these 'friends' is somewhat suspect, I discover, as I surf through endless postings filled with 'shout-outs', 'whazups' and liberal sprinklings of heart and unicorn icons, to find comments that reveal only a handful of friends with any actual real-life connection to Taylor.

My focus narrows to the portion of Taylor's page where she describes her favourite reading material. A questionnaire poses the query 'What's your favourite book?' She answers with a question: 'Does *Teen Vogue* count?' I rub my temples, reach for the paracetamol bottle, pop the cap and continue on. From what we know about Taylor through her profile, she's an avid fashionista and clothes shopper most likely to buy her clothes in boutique shops within a large shopping mall outside her small town.

But I'm getting ahead of myself. Perhaps I should pause at this point and answer the question as to why a normal forty-year-old heterosexual male is spending this particular Monday morning creating Taylor's persona from various MySpace pages, trying to understand teen media consumption and fashion sense.

The story begins in a temporary office space of a nondescript office building in Redwood Shores, California, where, with a full day of meetings, deadlines and administrative tasks on my to-do list, I put everything on hold as I stared at the screen in front of me. There must be something wrong here, I thought. How could the search query 'prom dresses' be one of the top search terms for US Internet users in January?

While on any given day I may be commenting on the state of online retail, the latest stats for Google or the demographics for visitors to online travel sites, I live for days like today. Confronted with a single enigmatic data point, I dive headfirst into a massive database to unravel the mystery behind something that my common sense tells me is out of place. Sometimes my data detours take less than an hour (can I predict an *American Idol* or *Dancing with the Stars* winner from search-term data?), or less than a day (what effect do rising petrol prices have on interest in hybrid vehicles?); sometimes they can occupy an entire year and cross several continents – and such was the case with the mystery surrounding searches for 'prom dresses'.

The blinking red message light on my phone reminded me that I had other pressing matters, but what was really demanding my attention at that second was on my screen, the twenty-third most popular search term of nearly 1 million terms driving traffic to retail sites for the month of January. I had given one of my research analysts an assignment to comb through the list of search terms that send traffic to the 22,000-plus websites that we track in the Retail category, to find patterns in search behaviour.

Having examined search-term behaviour for years, we know that many Internet users employ search engines as a means to navigate the Web, by searching for domains such as 'ebay.com' or 'www.ebay.com'. These domain-based searches always appear on top of any list of searches performed by Internet users. In the number twenty-three position, 'prom dresses' was the first non-navigational term, a fact that was quite puzzling given the fact that the prom season was in May.

One of the tactics that I use when confronted with a counterintuitive data point is to seek confirmation of that data point from other sources. I quickly looked through our database of 1,400 Hitwise customers and located some apparel designers and department stores. I also quickly researched some contact numbers for prom dress designers and sites specializing in prom apparel. After thirty minutes of phone calls to those supposedly in-the-know in the prom dress industry, the retailers that I spoke to had all agreed that there was something off about our data, as they all structure their advertising and merchandising around prom season (March–May).

Still perplexed, and as a visual thinker, I decided to generate a chart of the volume of searches for 'prom dresses' over a two-year period; it corroborated the same spike that we were seeing in the search-term list, a massive surge in January two years running. As I grabbed my second cup of coffee for the morning, I was perplexed. Shouldn't our Internet behaviours be somewhat consistent with the way we behave in the real world? Why would the Internet universe entertain searches for prom dresses in January?

My attention turned back to Taylor, my devised persona, another research tool that we use in understanding customers and creating a marketing plan that's appropriate for the person a client is trying to attract. Throughout my career in market research, I've found it's inevitable that if you spend enough time in the data, you can lose sight of your objective. Often when I'm confronted with a seemingly insoluble problem, I'll exercise my right brain by creating

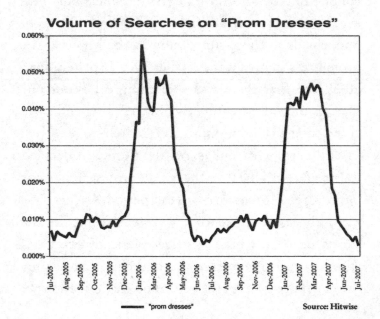

Volume of Searches on "Prom Dresses"

"prom dresses"   Source: Hitwise profiles of today's Internet user based on behaviour patterns. In this case, I go from the macro question 'Prom in January?' down to something real and tangible by creating a profile of today's prom-obsessed teenager. By creating the persona of Taylor, perhaps I could find some reasons behind the discrepancies between our data and what the prom dress industry was telling me.

To create Taylor, I started with the simple search query 'prom dresses'. Using our database of search behaviour, I pulled the most popular site visited when someone entered the term 'prom dresses' into a search engine in the second week of January. The site in the number one position for that week was www.promgirl.net. The PromGirl website sells a collection of designer dresses and offers content articles on upcoming fashion and prom resources, including links to things like acne treatments.

I had another very powerful tool at my disposal, a system that segments the US population into sixty-six parts based on behavioural data such as store purchases, magazine subscriptions, media behaviours and survey responses. This data, compiled by Claritas, a service of the Nielsen Company, is known as the PRIZM segmentation. By applying the PRIZM segments to our data, which our data partners provide by appending codes based on Zip + 4, we're able to analyse the segment-by-segment breakdown in visits to more than 35,000 different websites in the United States. Claritas also groups these segments into Lifestage Groups (which group people by where they are in their lives: younger years, family years or mature years) and Social Groups (which provide insight into where people live: urban, suburban, small city, town or rural area). Since a chart of visits to PromGirl.net revealed the identical pattern to searches on 'prom dresses' (visits spike during January), by analysing the psychographic segmentation of visitors to that site I could get a picture of the typical household in which we might find our teen persona Taylor.

So by following the trail from searches on search engines, to individual sites, and the segments visiting those sites, we could tell that in the month of January the most popular social group for visits to PromGirl. net was the affluent rural group, labelled T2, or the 'Country Comforts'. ('T' denotes a rural segment, while the '2' is a measure of affluence, 1 being the most affluent and 4 being the least.)

To build my profile of Taylor, I went back to the Claritas database to find a county in the United States that had one of the highest concentrations of Country Comforts. I settled for a quiet rural area in eastern Virginia bordering Chesapeake Bay. With a quick Google search I identified the top high schools in the area, then searched the profiles on MySpace for current students of those high schools, and with a minimal amount of effort I had before me a rich set of profiles of Country Comforts prom attendees. The profiles were data-rich, including everything from favourite music to favourite television shows and stores, as well as time- and date-stamped banter between friends on a variety of topics, including, among other things, the upcoming prom.

While viewing these various profiles, I got the sense that the prom industry had changed significantly since my time at school. I opened up another tab in my browser and pulled some numbers on the market size of the business. I was surprised to discover how big it actually is: according to the International Formal Association (IFA), a more than $4-billion-per-year business to be exact. The IFA estimates that, today, the average teen couple spends in excess of $1,200 on dinner, limousine, corsage, hair, tuxedo and . . . prom dress. While I can't speak for the cost of my date's dress, in 1984 I rented a tuxedo ($40), borrowed my parents' car ($10 in petrol), showed up at her door with a corsage ($10), and dinner was included in the prom tickets ($40 each). I spent a total of $140.[8] Times have changed. In fact, according to the IFA, the average female prom attendee will try on more than thirty-three dresses in the weeks leading up to the big event.

Comfortable in the potential business application of this exercise, I sought to answer the primary question. If most proms take place in mid-to-late May, why would the highest volume of searches for 'prom dresses' occur in the first week in January? I reverted back to charting searches on the term. The initial chart I had drawn on prom dress search patterns looked at all searches in the United States regardless of their end destination. By breaking down the chart into different end destinations, I could begin dissecting the user intent behind these searches. For example, if we charted searches on 'prom dresses' that resulted in users visiting specialty apparel and fashion sites, we got an entirely different pattern than if we charted those searches that resulted in visits to more general online department store sites. When I first created the Taylor persona, one of the commonalities in those that fit the description was a stated interest in fashion magazines; given that interest, it was likely that she would be among the group that began prom dress searches in January, shortly after reading about the upcoming fashions in their favourite magazines.

There is a very different search curve for visits that end up in general department store sites; these searches conform to a more expected surge in mid-April. If there are two separate search patterns, it's likely that there are two different behaviour segments, which likely represent two types of prom attendees and the need for a second profile.

Unlike Taylor, a prom fashionista, the mid-April prom dress searcher is more likely to search for price-conscious terms such as 'cheap prom dress', and would be likely to visit a site like www.edressme.com, where in mid-April the most prominent PRIZM demographic is less affluent suburban households known as S3, or the 'Middleburbs' At this point I introduced my second prom dress persona, 'Cassie'.

Standing in line at a Starbucks, you would have little difficulty distinguishing between these two teens (household members in the Country Comforts and Middleburbs are both likely to frequent Starbucks) as they order their Banana Caramel Frappuccinos.

Unlike the fashion-forward Taylor, our second amalgamated teen, from the Middleburbs, is more of a prom utilitarian. Cassie lives in a single-parent home in a small suburb outside Orlando, Florida. Like Taylor, Cassie loves shopping; however, her taste in clothing tends to be more practical and affordable. On her MySpace page Cassie lists her favourite shops as Abercrombie & Fitch and Hollister.

Also unlike Taylor's page, which appears to represent teen utopia, Cassie's page is an outlet for teen angst. Her page's background music is an angry heavy-metal piece with lyrics that I can't quite discern. The music, however, seems to be a fitting accompaniment to her blog entries, which express hatred for her father, who left the home when Cassie was very young, and general distrust boys, who, according to her dark Goth-themed profile, 'only want one thing'.

For Cassie, prom is just another party during the school year and an un-hip one at that. In fact, Cassie clearly states her proclivity for Cuervo Gold and tanning booths, which seems oddly out of character for her Goth personality. (I associate 'Goth' with pale skin, hair dyed black, and clove cigarettes.) Her Internet behaviour while revealing a darker, more troubled childhood than Taylor's, also reveals a more price-conscious prom dress search mission, which would probably begin in late March or early April. For Cassie, prom is more of a necessity, an event she plans to attend with like-minded friends, than something she's been planning all year. Prom dresses in this case are a low-consideration purchase. She'll most likely be buying her dress at a department store in the local shopping mall after researching basic styles and prices on the Internet.

While we may have always known about the differences between these two types of teens, Internet browsing data combined with psychographic purchase behaviour provides us with detail of their different lives, but perhaps most importantly helps us explain why prom dress searches (at least for some girls) reach their peak in January.

As I've come to learn from dissecting Internet trends over the years, the first of the year is a very peculiar time on the Internet, a virtual sandbox of introspection, organization and resolutions. Top-of-mind topics can range from losing weight and getting fit to smoking cessation and even pregnancy. (I never thought of pregnancy as a New Year's resolution, a detour I'll cover in Chapter 4.)

How we search and browse the Internet can tell us a lot about ourselves, and prom dresses are a simple example of that. While we assume that what happens in the offline world is mirrored in the online world, often that's not the case. The availability of massive amounts of online user behaviour data reveals not only the difference between the two worlds, but also the subtleties of our interests and thoughts at any given time.

To date, understanding societal behaviours, preferences and responses to stimuli has been an inexact science at best. Researchers have had to rely on either empirical data or primary research data gathered through surveys to understand our society, though both of these tools have limitations. Empirical data, while relying on observed behaviour, is not very cost-efficient to gather unless the data already exists that specifically addresses the question you're trying to answer.

The expansion of the Internet into our daily lives and the replacement of tasks in the real world with their online counterparts have an interesting by-product. How often do you search online for a phone number versus turning to the white or yellow pages of the phone book to look up a number? How often do you send a quick email versus writing and posting a letter? Are you more likely to make travel plans online than to pick up the phone and talk to a travel agent or reservationist? As this substitution of online for offline activities continues, a rich set of observed data is amassed that gives us insight into what we do during our daily lives. This insight can go beyond simple ups and downs in search-term data, into the actual intent behind those searches.

For example, by observing Internet use, we can gain insight into how things such as the onslaught of information from television, print and even the Internet itself can change behaviour.

Consider how much the Internet has changed prom dress shopping. Prior to the Internet, the prom dress shopping season was dictated by the retailer. Upcoming prom fashions would begin showing up in shops in late March at the earliest. With the advent of the Internet, prom fashion merchandise and information is available $24 \times 7 \times 365$.

While I could understand girls like Taylor searching for prom dresses so early in the season, I was still baffled by the pattern that represented all prom dress searches by all teen Internet users. Was the first week of January, on average, really the height of the prom dress season?

On occasion, when I'm on the road speaking, I've been known to place one of these charts into my presentation on the off chance that someone in the audience might have a clue to help me solve the mystery. I took my chances with the prom dress chart at a breakfast presentation for the Online Publishers Association. At the end of my presentation a very distinguished gentleman approached me as I was disconnecting my computer from the projector. He said, 'I'm all about prom dresses, and I think I know the answer to why you're seeing that January spike.' I stopped what I was doing. I looked at the business card that he had just handed to me. I was speaking to the general manager of the online teen division of a major publisher. He told me that the teen print media and the addition of the Internet to the equation have changed users behaviour over the last several years. Years ago the advertising season for prom was between March and May. But to lengthen the advertising season – prom being the most lucrative advertising season for teen fashion magazines – the industry has been putting out prom fashion editions in late December. Over time these factors changed user behaviour so that girls are looking for prom dress fashions online as early as January.

Indeed, copies of *Cosmo Girl Prom* and *Seventeen Prom* have been hitting the stands at the beginning of the New Year, to be purchased by the likes of Taylor and her friends, setting the fashion trends for the coming year. As a result, a certain segment of teens have been conditioned to begin thinking about prom a full five months in advance. Seeing that counterintuitive graph of prom dress searches in January was my first clue to this shift.

Certain aspects of prom timing remain the same, however. To put this all in perspective, I charted searches on 'prom dresses', 'prom hairstyles', and 'tuxedos' on the same chart. Assuming that hair issues are probably more likely to cause a flurry of activity closer to prom season, we can see how early dress searches actually occur when compared to searches for last-minute preparation.

If you're wondering if teen boys are as involved in prom research, we can answer that by charting tuxedo searches during the same time frame. Tuxedo searches are an order of magnitude smaller than their prom dress counterparts. To widen the gap between the sexes even more, by looking at the sites visited from those searches we can see that more than 50 per cent of visitors to the top tuxedo sites are female. This demographic discrepancy could be explained by a likely mixture of prom dates and moms conducting these searches. Regional data on site visitors can tell us even more.

For example, proms are *big* in the South. One of the most popular prom queries on the Internet is for 'plus size prom dresses'. These searchers are most likely to visit www.sydneyscloset.com, a site that claims to 'size-up glamour'. Interestingly, visitors to this site are most likely to come from Mississippi, Louisiana, North Carolina or Georgia. Having spent much time in the South, I can only guess that this is a phenomenon related to good, down-home Southern cooking.

Not all prom dress searches or searchers are created equal. I began to analyse the most common phrases that contained 'prom dresses'. The data revealed many ways that we could group these searches, from colour, to designer, to sizing issues, to price.

For our purposes, let's stick to a very simple categorization of two different types of searches: those that revolve around the research of prom dress fashion and those that are purchase-related.

If we scrutinize the surge in searches that happens in January every year, what we find is that these searches are focused on researching the fashion trends for the upcoming season. January searches contain designer phrases like 'tiffany prom dress', 'alyce prom dresses' and 'xcite prom dresses'. We can imagine Taylor in this early season mix, and actually catch snippets of discussion in the comment section

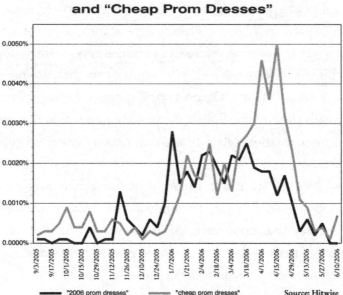

Volume of Searches on "2006 Prom Dresses" and "Cheap Prom Dresses"

Source: Hitwise

of her profile. Later in the season, however, between March and April, we find that girls like Cassie are engaging in more practical searches for 'cheap prom dresses', 'discount prom dresses', and 'low cost prom dresses.' Along these same lines, in the beginning of the year prom dress searches drive visits to fashion sites, while later in the year these same searches are more likely to send traffic to online department stores.

Aside from helping to solve the puzzle of what appeared to be erroneous data, this exercise provides a great example of just how the Internet has changed our purchase behaviours, not only for prom dresses but also for industries like fashion publishing, whose editors can now extend the prom fashion season into a five-month period. What is most striking about the prom dress phenomenon is that while fashion magazine editors and designers were aware of the trend, the shift in timing escaped the notice of retail outlets that carried prom attire. This differential in awareness created inefficiency in the online marketplace. Had marketers been paying attention to search trends, they might have captured the attention of prom shoppers at the beginning of their purchase research. In addition to pointing out the inefficiency, the exercise also provides the fashion industry with a means to extend this phenomenon beyond US borders.

PROM DRESSES CROSS THE POND

In the summer of 2005 I had the pleasure of speaking to a capacity crowd in London on the role of competitive intelligence in the search field. Knowing of my fascination with prom dresses, and the nature of the prom as an American tradition, I was asked by my UK marketing manager, Jannie Cahill, to stay away from the topic, for fear of alienating my audience of Brits. Of course, such a request was almost an assurance that the topic would appear within my keynote speech.

On a whim, the day before I was to speak I researched the volume of searches for 'prom dresses' in the United Kingdom. To my surprise, the chart revealed a significant number of searches on the term, and the pattern of searches was nearly identical to a US prom dress chart.

A little puzzled at this trend, I found the site receiving the most traffic on prom terms, www.teentoday.co.uk, and called the phone number listed in the 'about us' section of the site. Oliver Meakings, the site's editor, was eager to shed insight into how an American tradition had crossed the pond. According to Ollie, teens in the UK have end-of-year dances to celebrate the conclusion of the school year. Over the last few years the proliferation in UK cable screenings of American television shows such as *Beverly*

Top 20 Search Phrases in the United States and UK That Contain "Prom" (Week Ending 6 May 2006)

US Top 20	Per cent Share
prom dresses	11.02%
prom hairstyles	6.69%
prom hair styles	3.18%
prom hair	2.55%
prom updos	2.31%
prom	2.27%
prom dress	1.22%
cheap prom dresses	1.13%
prom shoes	1.09%
hairstyles for prom	0.82%
hair styles for prom	0.63%
tiffany prom dresses	0.58%
2006 prom dresses	0.54%
prom hairdos	0.54%
2006 prom hairstyles	0.52%
pictures of prom hairstyles	0.46%
prom hair dos	0.43%
sexy prom dresses	0.33%
prom 2006	0.31%
prom gowns	0.31%

UK Top 20	Per cent Share
prom dresses	19.85%
prom hairstyles	4.11%

UK Top 20 (continued)	Per cent Share
prom dress	3.45%
prom hair styles	2.10%
prom	1.81%
prom hair	1.46%
prom dresses uk	1.45%
prom shoes	1.43%
cheap prom dresses	0.74%
prom suits	0.47%
prom dress hire	0.47%
prom dress uk	0.32%
prom dresses in uk	0.28%
prom dresses in the uk	0.22%
designer prom dresses	0.22%
fashion show games prom	0.22%
prom dresses shops in london	0.20%
uk prom dresses	0.20%
prom jewellery	0.20%
prom wear	0.20%

Source: Hitwise

Hills 90210 and the more recent *The OC* has caused British teens to assimilate the prom tradition into their own culture.

Examining the 'prom' search terms for both the United States and the UK, we find that there is a great deal of similarity between the two in the top searches. But that's where the similarity ends. In the

United States hair is apparently a major cause for concern during May, while in the UK late searches are still focusing on the basics, like where to buy a prom dress. The other notable difference between the United States and the UK in prom searches is that gents in England are a little more involved than their American counterparts. The term 'prom suits' appears in the number ten position in the UK list, while 'tuxedo' is nowhere to be found in the US top list.

THE 'OTHER' DRESS AND THE ENGAGEMENT ULTIMATUM

Prom dresses do not provide the only enlightening pattern that we can find in search-term data. Serendipity led us to wedding dress searches and their link to engagement ring queries. 'Wedding dresses' are the second (but distant) most popular 'dress' query on the Internet, and by no coincidence, like 'prom dresses', they also peak at the first of the year. As with 'tuxedos', an analysis of the top search terms containing 'wedding' confirms that this event has little to do with the groom, who doesn't show up in the search terms until a reference occurs in the 145th term, for 'men's wedding ring'.

While there are additional search spikes for 'wedding dresses' during the week of Valentine's Day and the beginning of the wedding season in early June, the January timing for wedding dress searches is not surprising, if you consider that these searches are most probably related to proposals occurring on either Christmas or New Year's Day, two of the most common proposal days of the year.

A chart of 'wedding dresses' against 'engagement rings' searches corroborates the theory. The surprise was discovering that there were massive spikes in searches for engagement rings in the week before Thanksgiving; in fact, searches for engagement rings during this week were more than double the normal level.

Two theories come to mind to explain why this marked increase in interest occurs a week before retail stores see their surge in sales. First, the practical explanation: The pre-Thanksgiving spike reflects research-related queries. Since, for large purchases, the Internet is used primarily as a research tool, it's reasonable to expect that would-be proposers would research their large purchase the week before going into a store and buying a ring.

The more pessimistic theory, as put forth by my research analyst LeeAnn Prescott, is that Thanksgiving is a family holiday, and a likely time that a girl would bring her serious boyfriend home to meet the parents. Prior to the trip, 'the talk' occurs, where girl asks boy where the relationship is going, possibly issuing an ultimatum: Either propose before meeting my parents or we're through. There is a 'convenient excuse' variation to the engagement ultimatum, and that is that the boy, wanting to ask the girl's father for permission to marry his daughter, uses Thanksgiving as a convenient excuse to research engagement rings online, ask the parents and then pop the question on New Year's Eve.

This highlights a dichotomy in the research behaviours around two different items. Prom dresses are most likely researched by females in a research cycle that can span four to five months, for a dress that might cost between $200 and $300, compared to searches for engagement rings, most probably one of the largest lifetime purchases for a man, but with a research window of a single week. This, by the way, is just the beginning of our observations of the differences between men and women online.

In September 2001 the jewellery industry noticed an unseasonable increase in sales of engagement rings immediately following 9/11. In a time of national tragedy, such as the attacks of that day, while it's intuitive that flag sales would be up 1,800 per cent compared to the previous year and ammunition sales up over 100 per cent,[9] the increase in engagement ring sales was a little more puzzling. The 9/11 effect demonstrated that an attack on American soil, something not experienced by most Americans in their lifetime till then, while causing an outpouring of patriotism and in some cases vigilantism, could also cause us to look inward. An event that left the entire country with a sense of anger, and some with the need for revenge, also left us with a sense of emptiness. As was discovered in the unusual engagement ring sales figures from jewellers across the country, 9/11 left many with a need to connect and find strength in one another's company.

In our analysis of the holiday season of 2005, the November engagement ring pattern of the previous two years did not recur. Going backwards, however, we found that there had been an unseasonable rise in engagement ring searches in the first part of September. Wedding dress queries spiked in that very same week. It was the week following the devastating strike of Hurricane Katrina.

When it comes to online interest, timing can be elusive, and it can change. For example, in the last year the rise in prom dress queries has moved all the way back to November/December. What becomes clear over time, as I talk to marketers in various fields, is that miscalculation of online interest based on our instinct about that timing is almost universal. Watching consumers' actual online behaviour is the surest way to keep abreast of every changing consumer use, and to understand what is important and when.

CHAPTER 4

Failed Resolutions and the False Hope Syndrome

The first week of January is a peculiar time when it comes to analysing Internet behaviour. While there is plenty of search and visit activity around traditional New Year's resolutions such as losing weight, getting in shape and kicking the smoking habit, some searches reveal that the first week of the year is also a time of deep introspection and planning.

That interest in examining our lives and what lies ahead for the coming year has meaning beyond discovering when we're interested in a particular subject or item. At times our searches reveal a little glimpse into the human condition, our weaknesses and frailties. I would have to admit that I found some comfort when examining some of the data around New

Year's resolutions and seeing the short-term nature of our resolve to change.

To explain the value of search-term data in providing insight into what we're all about, I have one chart that I'm likely to put into a PowerPoint deck regardless of whether I'm speaking at a retail conference, travel convention or any other industry gathering. Usually I put the chart up without any titles or indication of what I'm actually charting. I then ask the audience to guess what I'm showing. After a few guesses that vary by venue, I reveal that I'm showing the pattern of searches on 'diets' in the United States.

The interesting part is that once I point out that fact, most of the audience can then identify the high points and low points without looking at the dates on the x axis. Most of us have either struggled with weight issues and diet misinformation or we know someone who has.

The ads are hard to miss: 'Lose 20 pounds in 4 weeks,' 'Lose 10 pounds in just 3 days,' 'Lose weight, no exercise, no dieting, no pills!' With the volume of extreme, outrageous claims that bombard us by email and through advertisements on search engines and in banner ads on websites, it's remarkable that obesity in America has reached epidemic proportions affecting nearly 60 million Americans.

The first thought that enters my mind when I see these claims is that everyone would be thin if losing weight were this easy. Yet the persistence of these ads year in and year out, combined with our expanding waistlines, is proof that we continue to fall for spurious claims – and the damage may be far worse. Could it be that these advertisements go beyond being useless, over-exaggerated advertising and actually increase the likelihood of our falling off the food wagon? Perhaps outrageous diet ads do the opposite of what they claim, ultimately exacerbating our weight issues.

Internet data tells us that, like most of our dieting patterns, interest in diets online yo-yos from predictable highs to predictable lows each year. And thanks to search marketing, these extreme dieting claims surface when we consult a search engine on the best way to lose weight.

For a brief period of time, four days at the beginning of the New Year to be exact, there is a surge in weight loss and fitness interest (and coincidentally, online and search engine marketing). Estimates are that between 40 and 45 per cent of all Americans make New Year's resolutions each year, but only 46 per cent report keeping their resolutions past six months.[10] (Although, as we learned in the previous chapter, the concept of cognitive dissonance gives significant cause to doubt even that claim. After all, who wants to admit to themselves, never mind to a surveyor, that he or she didn't have the willpower to keep New Year's resolutions?)

With such a gloomy outlook on our chances for successfully keeping a New Year's resolution like losing weight, why do we approach each successive start of the year with such gusto and commitment to finally make a change? The answer might lie in the sense of control, albeit very brief, that New Year's resolutions give us. I have the power to change; I can take control of my life, my weight, fitness or finances. But each successive failure, each new attempt backed by even bolder claims of our ability to radically change our lives, fuels hope that eventually leads to failure – or 'false hope syndrome'.

Janet Polivy, a professor of psychology at the University of Toronto, coined that phrase to describe the results of her research. False hope syndrome is the sorry state of our persistent attempts at change despite previous failures. Dr Polivy reasons that the act of simply making a commitment to change provides us with a temporary sense of control that overtakes our memory of past failed attempts. The sense of control is short-lived, and the more unrealistic our dieting expectations, the greater the fall.

In a study at the University of Toronto, a group of eighty-seven women participated in an experiment involving the effects of unrealistic dieting claims on their commitment to change. In the study, the women were first separated into three groups, then each group was shown one of three different levels of weight loss ads, with three differing levels of dieting claims, from 'lose twelve pounds in one week', to 'lose six pounds in one week', to 'lose up to two pounds in one week'.

At the onset of the experiment, the women were told that they were going to be participating in two different studies (although the two activities were actually part of the same experiment). After being shown the ads, they were to participate in a biscuit tasting study. Each of the three groups was escorted to a different room, where large plates of biscuit awaited them. At the end of a ten-minute tasting period, when the study participants had left the rooms, all the plates of biscuits were weighed. The weight of each room's biscuits plates revealed clear differences among the groups. Could it be that the ads tested in the first half of the experiment actually affected the short-term eating habits of the participants?

The data indicates that they did. The group shown the ad with the most aggressive dieting claims ate the fewest number of cookies, while the group shown the ad with the least fantastic claims ate the most.

This experiment demonstrates the response that is elicited from us when we think we have the opportunity for dramatic change in our lives. The eagerness of the group expecting to 'lose twelve pounds in one week' is probably related to their feelings of control and exuberance. Unfortunately, since most of these claims either require unrealistic restrictions on calorie intake or are wholly unsubstantiated, they usually lead ultimately to failure and disappointment – what Dr Polivy termed the false hope syndrome.

Looking at our Internet usage habits around what should be the official holiday for false hope syndrome, 1 January or New Year's Day, we can see this exuberance towards life-change play out, both in the dramatic increase in searching for information on dieting and weight loss, and in the subsequent loss of interest as we realize that our initial goals were unrealistic.

What can Internet data reveal about false hope syndrome and our lack of willpower?

Internet browsing and search-term data reveal a lot about our psyche and this short-lived sense of being able to control our lives and execute our commitments to change. In the Internet age, diet awareness may be the result of online advertising, or something that happens offline, like a television or radio commercial, both of which ultimately drive us to find out more; and the means of looking for that information is most likely to be a search engine. By monitoring aggregate search activity, we see the patterns play out.

Every 1 January, as bookshops fill their front tables with dieting, fitness and home improvement books, as gyms aggressively pursue the resolved, search engines show a predictable and impressively large spike of queries on betterment issues. Here I plotted searches for 'Thanksgiving recipes' alongside online dieting visits to show the juxtaposition of our greatest food holiday with the low point in dieting interest.

Not only are the search spikes impressive, but the yearly pattern of visits to online dieting sites is one of the most predictable in the realm of all Internet behaviour. Every year, the peak for visits to sites that

Visits to Online Dieting Sites and Searches for "Thanksgiving Recipes"

online dieting — Thanksgiving recipes — Source: Hitwise

help users develop dieting plans online occurs on the first day of the new year. That peak in interest lasts only between four and five days. By the fifth day of January, visits to dieting sites begin a steep slide that won't show any increases until summer, when there will be renewed dieting interest for bathing suit season.

In fact, by charting dieting and bikini searches together, we can see that we're thinking in advance, as early as March and April of each year, before the need arises for swimwear, with bikini searches acting as a great proxy for swimsuit interest, which begins in late May and ends in the August time frame.

Volume of Searches on "Diets" and "Bikini"

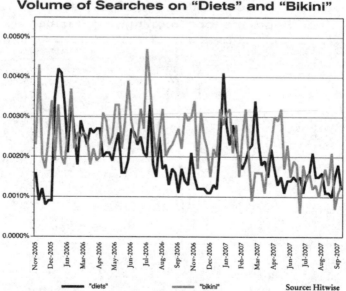

As soon as our interest in looking better for the summer beach season concludes, dieting interest begins to take another dive, to reach the lowest point of the year, the day when most of us are in the greatest need for nutritional guidance, or better yet, control, the holiday with the greatest maximum caloric intake . . . Thanksgiving Day.

The fact that the chart shows that New Year's Day is the peak for visits to dieting sites or searches on diets is not surprising to anyone. When my Power-Point lands on this particular chart during a presentation, the audience is sure to laugh, as well as instantly become engaged in the idea that we can learn more about ourselves through our Internet behaviour.

At the end of every presentation, I'm bound to get a few questions, either in a Q&A period or afterwards from those who prefer to ask their questions one-on-one. At a search-engine conference in New York, one of the audience members approached me after the presentation for the sole purpose of telling me how much she enjoyed the dieting chart. I took the opportunity to ask why this chart out of the forty or so that I had shown that morning was so interesting, and she replied that it was a very obvious chart, but it was comforting to see that dieting patterns that she had experienced herself, her own false hope syndrome, were not hers alone but shared by a large portion of the sample that I monitor.

Another source of feedback is my blog (www. ilovedata.com), where my analyst team posts our favourite data points and analyses. One very astute reader pointed out an interesting variation in dieting queries in late 2005.

In the chart that my blog reader sent over, of diet website visits, there was an increase in visits to dieting sites from September to November 2005 that didn't exist in 2004. By looking at the changes in diet searches surrounding this unseasonable spike, we began to dig into the reasons for the increase. Starting with the top websites in our Wellness category (where all of our dieting sites reside), there were a number of sites appearing within the top ten that had not been there in the previous year.

Expanding our focus beyond website visits to search terms sending traffic to Wellness sites, we could see several new terms, such as 'Jillian Michaels,' 'Biggest Loser', and 'Biggest Loser Club', referring to the hit NBC reality series *The Biggest Loser,* a show where overweight contestants vie for a big cash prize based on their weight loss during the show. The show was confirming a paradoxical relationship between television (long blamed as a culprit in our losing battle against obesity) and our interest in fitness. Ironically, the week of Thanksgiving, viewers watching the season finale of *The Biggest Loser* were compelled to get off the couch and go to their computer to find out more about getting fit.

Over the last several years we've seen Internet use challenge television for our attention. An IBM Consumer Digital Media Report found that 'Among consumer respondents, 19 per cent stated spending six hours or more per day on personal Internet usage, versus 9 per cent of respondents who reported the same levels of TV viewing. Sixty-six per cent reported viewing between one to four hours of TV per day, versus 60 per cent who reported the same levels of personal Internet usage.'[11] Along with the rise of Internet use, online data shows, with increasing occurrence, that television programming is driving us to our computers to find out more about television shows and commercials that we've just watched. The drive from tube to laptop can be very direct, such as online contests that mirror their television counterparts, or it can be very subtle, as is the case with product placement.

With the rapid adoption of digital video recorders or DVRs, which enable viewers to fast-forward through blocks of commercials even during a real-time broadcast, television programmers and advertisers have sought ways of embedding advertising within the programme itself to preserve the ability to advertise to their couch-bound audience. According to research from Sanford Bernstein, the widespread use of DVRs will lead to the loss of more than $18 billion in advertising revenues by 2009.[12] The practice of product placement, or embedding products and services in programming for a fee, is an advertising solution to counteract commercial-skippers.

The practice of embedding commercials within programming is not a new concept. One of the most successful early product placements was in the hit movie *ET* Steven Spielberg approached the Mars company about featuring M&Ms in the movie as ET's favourite confection. When Mars declined the offer, Spielberg moved on to the Hershey Company, which decided against using its flagship Hershey's Kisses in the movie but chose to place its lesser-known Reese's Pieces. Within two weeks of the movie's première, sales for Reese's Pieces had jumped by 65 per cent.

Janet Jackson's wardrobe malfunction during the 2003 Super Bowl caused one of the greatest one-week increases in visits to a music artist's official website. Incidentally, the brand with the greatest volume of searches around the 2006 Super Bowl was 'Candice Michelle'. Not sure who Candice Michelle is? She starred in the Go Daddy 'Wardrobe Malfunction' spot, soundly beating Pepsi, Budweiser, FedEx and other Super Bowl brand advertisers in online searches.

In the case of *The Biggest Loser,* NBC was able to affect one of the most steadfast patterns in online behaviour with a message that commitment, proper nutrition and an intense fitness routine are the keys to lasting weight loss. Each year's dieting search terms reveal the latest fad diets mixed with traditional weight loss programmes.

The dieting industry is a $40-billion-a-year business, a combination of diet programmes, weight loss clinics, books and other self-help materials. A good portion of that business is earned during the first few days of the new year, as we all come to terms with our resolve to change, as the table on page 111 demonstrates.

Comparison with the previous year's terms shows a standard influx of fad diet searches, a trend that reappears every New Year's Day. But in 2006 there was a noticeable change, with terms focused more on fitness, nutrition and NBC's new hit show.

Our Internet behaviour reveals the depths of our aspirations. We want to lose weight to look thinner. We want to be healthy. Of the most popular Internet searches that contain the phrase 'how to' (discussed in greater detail in Chapter 6), 'how to lose weight', 'how to gain weight' and 'how to lose weight fast' are among the top queries.

Our searches also reveal that we're looking for a quick fix, a magic pill that can help the weight just melt off our bodies. Of the top ten searches containing 'pills', six of those searches were for diet or weight-loss pills, including searches for 'alli diet pills' and 'phentermine pills', beating searches for 'birth control pills', 'pain pills', and 'sleeping pills'.

If we take all of this data together, it becomes apparent that we are a society that is increasingly fixated on finding instant gratification. The short-term nature of our interest in changing ourselves for the better reflects our limited attention span, which desires instantaneous change. Along with improvements in productivity, the Internet has fuelled our ability to have things when we want them: the latest news and financial information, as well as communication with friends, family and colleagues via mobile, BlackBerry, Twitter or Facebook status update. In an environment where everything is so readily available, spending an inordinate amount of time on a specific goal seems out of sync with our life's pace.

There are other triggers to change beyond the first week of the year. Tragic events, such as the loss of a celebrity to an illness linked to vice, can also drive us

Top 20 Search Terms in Lifestyle–Wellness Category (Week Ending 21 January, 2006)

Search Term	Per Cent Share
weight watchers	1.56%
south beach diet	0.80%
gnc	0.70%
24 hour fitness	0.53%
nutrisystem	0.48%
calorie counter	0.43%
curves	0.37%
jenny craig	0.36%
diets	0.35%
the biggest loser	0.34%
weight loss	0.34%
biggest loser	0.32%
hydroxycut	0.29%
bally total fitness	0.26%
weightwatchers.com	0.25%
atkins diet	0.23%
golds gym	0.23%
la fitness	0.22%
www.lightnfit.com	0.22%
glycemic index	0.21%

Source: Hitwise

to think of change. Unfortunately, as with resolutions, this type of change is also very short-lived.

* * *

DIETING AND FITNESS ARE examples of leading New Year's resolution searches. The second runner-up, which is a little bit harder to quantify, is smoking cessation. By looking through all search terms that included the word 'stop' during the first four weeks of the year, we created a start list for other New Year's resolutions. Searches for 'stop sweating' and 'stop snoring', the only other resolution-type searches in the top ten, were dwarfed by searches to help 'stop smoking', and specifically by pharmaceutical means: 'stop smoking drug', 'stop smoking shot' and 'stop smoking pill'.

New Year's search activity around the desire to quit smoking demonstrates the irrationality of resolutions. One of the primary reasons to give up smoking is to avoid the habit's health consequences, the primary concern being contracting lung cancer. Yet in terms of search behaviour there is little to no connection between searches on smoking cessation and searches on lung cancer. If you look at searches on 'stop smoking', you'll find that, like all good resolutions, searches remain relatively constant throughout the year but generally peak for New Year's. While there was no New Year's spike in 2006, there was significant interest in smoking cessation in April 2006, with the pending FDA approval of a new Pfizer drug that was shown to aid one in five smokers in the quest to kick the habit.

While 'stop smoking' searches generally increase in January, that's not the case with 'lung cancer' searches. As we have found with many other serious diseases, celebrities diagnosed with a disease can cause a dramatic increase in searches on the topic. In August 2005 Americans were stunned by the passing of ABC News anchor Peter Jennings at the age of sixty-seven from lung cancer. Jennings had only learned of his cancer diagnosis in April of that year; five months later, after a course of aggressive chemotherapy, he succumbed to the disease. Searches on the topic of lung cancer rose dramatically that week. Searches during that week containing 'lung cancer' included 'lung cancer symptoms', 'symptoms of lung cancer' and 'dana reeve lung cancer'.

Dana Reeve, widow of the late actor Christopher Reeve, disclosed that she suffered from lung cancer only two days after Jennings's death. Seven months later Reeve also succumbed to the disease. During that week in March 2006 searches on 'lung cancer' reached their highest point in three years, tripling their normal weekly volume.

The interesting point, however, is that with the deaths of Jennings and Reeve, our awareness of lung cancer increased but our interest in stopping the activity that is the leading cause of the disease didn't. Searches on 'stop smoking' were remarkably flat.

Could the fact that Reeve's rare case of contracting lung cancer without a history of smoking caused a sense of futility, resulting in no smoking cessation spike in March 2006? Or perhaps the lack of connection between 'lung cancer' searches and 'stop smoking' searches further demonstrates the principles of false hope syndrome. In January we feel a sense of control in resolving to change, and the desire to stop smoking in January may be driven more by this empowerment than by lung cancer concerns.

DIETING, STOPPING SMOKING, EXERCISING and getting organized are all traditional New Year's resolutions. But when we looked through the volumes of search-term data, certain patterns pointed to the existence of some untraditional resolutions. Like the resolution to get pregnant.

Did the mention of pregnancy as a New Year's resolution catch you offguard? Not something you normally think of when listing resolutions?

If we chart 'pregnancy' alongside 'wedding dress', 'fitness' and 'diet' queries, we see that the increase in searches for all of them happens in the first week in January. While 'wedding dresses' decreases immediately afterwards, 'pregnancy' queries continue to climb through the beginning of the year.

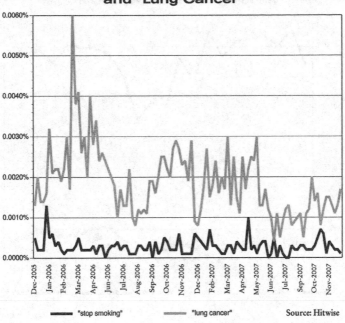

Volume of Searches on "Stop Smoking" and "Lung Cancer"

Beyond the obvious interpretations of a shotgun wedding or a *very* successful holiday proposal, there are two theories to account for this juxtaposition of terms. It could be a sign that mothers-to-be are considering the health of their unborn child in constructing a resolution. Some of the top baby sites optimize content at the beginning of the year for exactly that purpose, encouraging their readers to stop drinking and smoking, and get fit for the sake of their new baby. The second theory is that pregnancy

Volume of Searches on "Pregnancy", "Fitness", "Wedding Dresses" and "Diet"

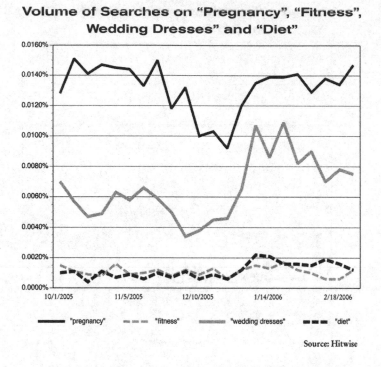

Source: Hitwise

itself is the resolution. By examining the search terms driving traffic to the most popular pregnancy websites, and the demographics of those sites, we can find evidence of the second theory in terms such as 'getting pregnant' rising to the top of the list at the beginning of the new year.

The most popular site visited from the search term 'pregnancy' is the site Pregnancy.org, which provides a resource for pregnant mothers or those considering getting pregnant. By examining the demographic composition of visitors to the site, we find a very interesting phenomenon. The composition of visitors grouped by age, gender and income level changes throughout the year. In the earlier days of the study of site demographics, it wasn't uncommon for a site to commission a study and then use those statistics for several years. Today, however, in the age of online competitive intelligence, we have discovered that demographics for a site can change drastically within a short period of time, often within a few weeks. And that's exactly the case with visits to Pregnancy.org.

The hypothesis behind the concept of pregnancy as a New Year's resolution is a relatively simple one. Within the last few decades the average age of a first pregnancy has steadily increased. This increase could be associated with the increase in dual household incomes, and the likelihood that both parents-to-be are focused on careers and delay starting a family or marrying until those aspirations are fulfilled. If behaviour patterns have shifted from the expectation that a couple begin to procreate immediately after marriage to the need to delay a family until financial security has been achieved, it's not too far-fetched to consider that some couples may take the first of the year as an opportunity to set a new goal for starting a family.

To test this hypothesis, I looked at the spread in age of visitors to the sites receiving the most traffic from the search term 'pregnancy': Pregnancy.org and About.com's pregnancy site (www.pregnancy.about.com). In comparing the autumn months with the first week of the new year I saw that the demographic spread of users did indeed vary significantly. For example, in September the percentage of 25–34-year-olds visiting Pregnancy.org numbered 39.4 per cent. In the first week of 2007 that same site received 48.4 per cent of its traffic from 25–34-year-olds, with 18–24-year-olds decreasing from 37 to 23 per cent. The same phenomenon occurred with About.com's pregnancy site, with 35–44-year-olds increasing from 12.7 per cent in autumn to 17.6 per cent in the first week of the year.

As was already mentioned, while studying the January pattern for pregnancy searches we noticed that 'wedding dresses' were another January phenomenon, which seemed odd. If we paid attention to the media (as we did in the altering of dieting patterns via NBC's *The Biggest Loser*), we would expect that the heavy coverage of wedding dress fashions in March would lead to a similarly timed spike in searches for wedding dresses. But as we saw in the previous chapter, that proves not to be the case. In retrospect, now that I understand media-conditioned behaviour, searches for 'prom dresses' or 'wedding dresses' in January make complete sense. Our Internet browsing behaviour may at first glance appear to be random and unconnected, but upon closer examination it reveals subtle but simple patterns of how we think and act.

In the case of our New Year's resolutions, as in other areas where we seek to better ourselves, the quick, get-it-now conditioning that Internet connectedness has provided us with has left us with a very limited attention span. In other words, I want what I want right now. The days of working for something are over. Today a long-term goal isn't measured in years or months, but a matter of days. Four to five to be exact.

While our attention span has shortened when it comes to self-improvement, our fascination with the lives of celebrities has grown significantly within the last several years. The flood of information about the daily lives of the rich and famous has caused an increase in the attention that we pay to our favourite stars. Our Internet behaviour can tell us the extent to which some of us have chosen to worship at the church of celebrity.

CHAPTER 5

Celebrity Worship Syndrome

Take any significant news story of the day, from the war in Iraq, to natural disasters such as tsunamis and earthquakes, to financial troubles such as sky-rocketing petrol prices, a falling housing market or the failure of sub-prime mortgages – each of these events pales in relation to one topic of online interest: the cult of celebrity personality. Floods, famine and poverty are no challenge to the obsession with Anna Nicole's death, the incarceration of Paris Hilton or even the news that *American Idol* contestant Antonella Barba may have posed for some racy pictures. Early in my Internet career I held various positions at search-engine companies. In those positions I was always amazed at the power of celebrity demonstrated in the searches that consumers typed into our engine. Within those searches I began to notice patterns; certain types of celebrity news trumped all others. Could these search spikes reveal why celebrity has become so important in our culture?

My curiosity about our celebrity focus continued when I took the role of general manager of global research for Hitwise. In fact, one of the 162 categories that we capture data on is the Entertainment-Personality category, which contains more than 800 celebrity-related sites. These sites combined garnered a relatively small percentage of all Internet visits, about 0.1 per cent during most of 2005 and 2006. But in November 2006 something changed.

In late 2006 the chart of visits to celebrity sites clearly showed an inflection point. Fuelled in part by the growth of celebrity blogs like PerezHilton. com and TMZ.com, and the amount of attention devoted to news around the death of Anna Nicole Smith in February 2007, visits to celebrity websites and sites devoted to celebrity news more than doubled by October 2007, only eleven months later, when the same set of sites accounted for 0.24 per cent of all Internet visits. To put that in perspective: In the United States celebrity websites garner more attention online than websites devoted to religion, politics and well-being (which includes the dieting sites), just to name a few.

Market Share of Visits to Entertainment-Personalities Category

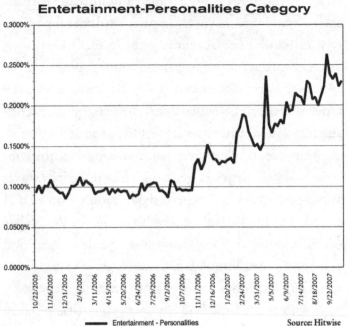

I've often wondered why, as a society, we are so fascinated by celebrities. I can remember examining databases of the most searched-for topic in the United States in late 2003. Despite everything going on in the world at the time, Paris Hilton in late 2003 (coincidentally just in time for the release of her reality television series with Nicole Richie, *The Simple Life*) became the most searched-for topic. Not just the most searched-for celebrity, but the most searched for topic in general. There are many reasons why we search for celebrities, but if you're looking for instant

Internet stardom, if you want to dominate searches across every major search engine, a scandalous celebrity sex tape is the quickest path. In fact today, four years after the release of her salacious footage on the Internet, Paris still receives 7.4 per cent of all 'sex tape' searches. The most searched-for phrase containing 'Paris Hilton' is 'Paris Hilton sex tape'.

While searching for compromising photos and videos of celebrities is growing in popularity (and it appears to be, based on the data, a male-dominated sport), the fascination with celebrities in general is much more pervasive, crossing gender, age, and socioeconomic boundaries. Early in my career at Hitwise I happened to meet Jim Houran, a psychologist, who at the time had the intriguing title of chief psychology officer for the dating site True Beginnings, which later became known as True. Several years later I ran across Jim's name as I researched the topic of celebrity fascination. Back in 2002 Houran, along with fellow researchers McCutcheon and Lange, developed a scale of the fascination that we have with public figures. They dubbed it the 'Celebrity Worship Scale'.

An enterprising British journalist coined his own phrase in reporting the research, calling it 'celebrity worship syndrome'. Jim Houran is quick to point out that his colleagues weren't adding to the already crowded collection of new syndromes, but rather had, through their research, identified a scale that measured how obsessed individuals were with celebrities. Over the years Jim's research spanned surveys of more than 20,000 respondents, and he found that all respondents identified with at least one of the three stages of celebrity worship. The first stage he calls the entertainment/social stage, a healthy interest in public figures that is a form of escapism, which also has a social component, where our interest in celebrities serves as social glue, giving us something to discuss at the office water cooler.

Houran identified a second stage, where the celebrity interest intensifies. This stage, the intense personal stage, is where we start to see the addictive components of celebrity worship, where individuals identify with statements like 'I believe my celebrity is my soul mate' and 'I have thoughts of my favourite celebrity even when I don't want to.' In the intense personal stage, individuals begin to show signs of withdrawing from society, finding fulfillment in stories about their favourite celebrity rather than interacting with the people around them.

The final, or borderline pathological, stage is where celebrity interest becomes an obsession. Respondents in this category endorsed statements like 'If my favourite celebrity asked me to do something illegal, I'd do it.' This is the stage where we might find the celebrity stalkers that make the news.

While there is little to no historical data on this phenomenon, with the Celebrity Worship Scale having been first devised in 2002, Houran thinks that celebrity worship is not a new phenomenon. As far back as we can remember, role models have played an important part in our society. The Internet, however, has served as a catalyst for our addiction. In pre-Internet days we satisfied our hunger for celebrity information through newspapers and magazines. Today the amount of information available on our favourite stars is staggering. Those in need of a star fix can find a nearly infinite amount of detail about their favourite celebrity by visiting the official website of their star, the online version of celebrity news magazines, countless entertainment blogs, and even, in some cases, blogs on specific individuals.

But what is it about celebrities that fascinates us most? If we look at the last several years we can see that there are certain events that cause dramatic spikes in celebrity searches. They are, in order of importance (measured by search volume): the leak of a celebrity sex tape, the death of certain celebrities (in death, not all celebrities are created equal), celebrities in trouble (either arrested or incarcerated), and then various celebrity news items, primarily those dealing with dating, marriage or newly born children.

Sex tape celebrity searches are clearly distinguishable from the rest of the pack in that, by tracing the way Internet users search for 'sex tapes' and their end destinations, we see that these searchers are primarily interested in finding the actual tapes and are predominately male. Still, it appears that our prurient interests are piqued when a celebrity romp is exposed, much more so than with any other type of pornographic content.

There are only certain celebrity deaths that lead to monumental spikes in search volume, the most recent and by far the most dramatic of those being the death of former *Playboy* playmate and subsequent reality television star Anna Nicole Smith. For the week ending 10 February 2007, the week of Anna Nicole's death, she became the fifth most popular search term of all US Internet searches that week reaching the highest point for any searched-on individual over the previous three years. During that week the top destination for searches on Anna Nicole was her official website, www.annanicole.com. By analysing the demographics and psychographics of visitors to her site that week, we can get a sense of just who was most fascinated with her untimely demise.

Born Vicki Lynn Marshall in 1967, Anna Nicole came from humble beginnings, dropping out of high school in Mexia, Texas, during her sophomore year. Anna Nicole's life reads more like an over-the-top movie script than even a Hollywood life story, from being a *Playboy* model and Playmate of the Year, to meeting her second husband, oil tycoon J. Howard Marshall, who was more than sixty years her senior. Bitter court battles ensued after Marshall's death, as she fought for her share of the $1.6 billion estate. With the untimely and suspicious death of her son only months before her own demise, it's no wonder that her death attracted curiosity, but could anyone have predicted the outpouring of interest? Looking at the search terms that contained 'Anna Nicole Smith' during the week of 10 February, we can see that there is evidence of disbelief, such as several queries that asked 'Is Anna Nicole dead?', and morbid fascination, as Internet users searched in the hope of finding 'pictures of Anna Nicole dead' and 'autopsy photos of Anna Nicole'.

One theory behind celebrity worship, and a possible explanation for our fascination with Anna Nicole's death, is that some celebrities garner more attention if society has found a way to identify with them. As Margaret Gibson stated in her editorial for *Mortality,* a professional journal covering issues surrounding death: 'In highly urbanized societies, with mass populations, most deaths are those of strangers, and these go unnoticed at the level of individual knowledge and concern. Many people can feel they know someone on television better than a neighbor or family member.'[13]

Indeed, prior to her death Anna Nicole was the star of her own reality television show, *The Anna Nicole Show*, where viewers were given a bird's-eye view of her bizarre dysfunctional life. Perhaps that connection, as well as the rags-to-potential-riches story that was Anna Nicole's life, was partly responsible for her posthumous superstardom. If that were true, one clue might be found in the demographics of visitors to the official Anna Nicole site in the week of her death in early 2007, as visitors would be those most likely to identify with her.

During the week of her death, the Anna Nicole website experienced more than an 8,000 per cent increase in visitors. According to the basic demographics, during that week, visitors to the site were predominately female (62 per cent), under the age of 44 (79 per cent), with the largest age group being 35–44-year-olds (29 per cent), in households earning below $60,000 per year (62 per cent). Psychographic profiles reveal that the most likely visitors to the site were the financially challenged Internet users in the Claritas PRIZM segment known as the 'Striving Singles', which is composed of 'twenty-something singles with low incomes working part-time service jobs while going to college'. In terms of geographical orientation, visitors to the site belonged to the least affluent rural group, known as 'Rustic Living', whose residents have 'modest incomes, low educational levels, aging homes, and blue-collar occupations'. Visitor data appears to corroborate the theory that those who might identify closest with Anna Nicole's beginnings were the ones most likely to feel the connection and seek closure on the Web.

Or perhaps it was simply the untimely nature of Anna Nicole's death that was the online draw for searches and visits to her site. Celebrity deaths have been known to draw out our fascination with the macabre. Within days of Steve Irwin's (the Crocodile Hunter) death from fatal wounds inflicted by a stingray barb in September 2006, searches on his name and his nickname soared. But, as with Anna Nicole Smith's autopsy photo searches, not all searches were focused on remembering Steve Irwin's life. Despite the fact that the only videotape of his death, taken by his film crew, was handed over to his widow, to this date searches persist for 'Steve Irwin's death video'.

Kofi Dwinfour, the senior marketing manager for A&E Television Networks, found a way to leverage our fascination with the macabre. In this new media world where traditional outlets are losing viewers and readers to the Internet, he is charged with finding synergies between the cable network channel and the company's Internet presence. After a session on using our data for customer acquisition, Kofi and I were talking about the Steve Irwin video chart. A&E airs a number of programmes on its cable network, including several shows that contain segments that are too gruesome to show on air. In the past, these segments ended up on the cutting-room floor. But given this new insight about just how insatiable our interest in gruesome content is, Kofi had an idea.

The network was airing a new show, *Gene Simmons: Family Jewels,* a follow-along reality series that shadowed KISS rock star Gene Simmons. In season two of the series Gene and his life partner, former *Playboy* playmate Shannon Tweed, undergo a couples face-lift. The network had already decided that some of the footage was too graphic to show on television. Connecting the dots, Kofi pitched the idea of messaging to TV viewers that some of the content was too graphic to show, but those who were interested could see an uncut version of the surgery coverage on the A&E website. After the show aired, viewers flooded the site. Kofi, leveraging our understanding of what drives consumer interest, created an ideal synergy between television and online content.

Another fascinating aspect of our celebrity obsession is the difference in celebrity websites visited by men as compared to women. When we look at those celebrity sites that have the greatest proportion of male visitors, they are sites like Egotastic.com and Propeller.com.

By visiting the Egotastic! website, you can clearly see a difference in the site as compared to celebrity websites in general. Egotastic! appears to specialize in provocative pictures of female celebrities. To confirm my suspicions, if we look at the search terms that Internet users are employing to arrive at the site, most are requests for provocative videos and pictures. The male fascination with female visuals is a phenomenon that shows up repeatedly in the data. My first finding in the area related to pictures, gender difference and online dating sites. At the time, in early 2005, we created a matrix of the top ten online dating sites and recorded, for each site, how long the registration process was, how expensive the fee was to join and maintain a membership, the length of any match-making surveys necessary, and finally whether the site permitted visitors to see free pictures of potential dates (versus requiring membership before viewing profile pictures).

We found that the more costly a site, the longer the registration and survey process, the more a site would skew towards female visitors. The one factor that would send a site skewing towards males was the availability to surf pictures prior to registering or joining the site's service.

If we examine the celebrity websites that have the largest percentage of women visitors, the list shows a clear bias towards the blogs that dish out gossip, sites like JustJared.buzznet.com, Bossip.com and of course PerezHilton.com. But what is striking about presumably female searches for male heart-throbs, stars like George Clooney and Matthew McConaughey, is that the searches aren't for pictures or videos of the stars, but for questions about their lives, specifically if they are married or dating anyone. For example, searches that contained 'George Clooney' for the four weeks ending 12 January included terms such as 'George Clooney girlfriend', 'Is George Clooney married?' and 'George Clooney solo red carpet', referring to a Clooney public appearance that was sans Sarah Larson (his girlfriend at the time). Do these searches indicate a fascination with stars' private lives or something more?

Searching on the hot female counterparts, stars like Jennifer Aniston, Angelina Jolie and Jessica Biel, we find that, unlike with their male counterparts, visuals dominate and there isn't a single mention of marital or dating status in queries containing the star's name.

In the second stage of the celebrity worship scale, Houran detailed how celebrity worshippers begin to exhibit an unrealistic identification with their chosen celebrity. If women are fantasizing about their favourite male star, and the key word is 'fantasizing', does it really matter if George Clooney is married or single? (After all, it is a fantasy.) Or perhaps some female Internet searchers, a large number based on search-term volume, are taking their fantasies to the next step – but only if their heart-throb is available.

IF I ASKED YOU where you consume your celebrity gossip online, your answer to that question would most probably depend on your age, your household income, whether you live in an urban, suburban, or rural area, and the specific region that you live in. For example, if you're 25–34 years old and live in an urban metropolitan area of the country, you're most likely to visit PerezHilton.com to get your daily celebrity gossip fix.

It's blogs like PerezHilton.com and TMZ.com that feed another interest of ours, the fascination with when bad things happen to the celebrities we follow. Whether it's the in-again out-again saga of Paris Hilton's imprisonment, the downfall of the latest teen star to alcohol, drugs or pregnancy, or stories about who dumped or hooked up with whom, celebrity blogs have become the replacement for the *National Enquirer*.

Perez Hilton – a pseudonym – was born Mario Lavandiera in Miami, Florida, the son of Cuban immigrants. After trying his hand at acting, Mario turned his attention to journalism. He started the blog Pagesixsixsix.com, which later would be called Perez Hilton.com, in 2004.[14] The site, which is best described as a photoblog with celebrity gossip, contains photos altered by Hilton to show cocaine residue and bodily fluid emissions in Wite-Out, like scribbling on top of existing photos of stars in the news. While the media depicts Perez Hilton as a personality who is loathed equally by Hollywood and by some gossip fans themselves, search-term data tells an entirely different story. Looking at the search terms associated with his name, it's clear that people are searching for Perez's coverage of the latest celebrity dirt.

Perez Hilton is a rising star in his own right, claiming the spot as the most popular blog visited on the Web (we count Web visits, not RSS feeds, which are a metric used to count those who read blogs through a separate blog reader). Since launching his site, Perez has reached and surpassed the top 500 of all websites visited in the United States. He also has become the most searched-for personality in the

Entertainment-Personalities category, garnering more searches than the likes of Oprah Winfrey, Howard Stern, Miley Cyrus and Kim Kardashian (a sex-tape-related search).

Visitors to the Perez Hilton site tend to be young (those aged 18–24 accounted for 35 per cent of his visitors), female (74 per cent) and affluent (with 33 per cent earning household incomes over $150,000 per year). In contrast to Anna Nicole's online mourners, visitors to Perez Hilton are in a whole different world. They are most likely to come from the most

Market Share of Visits to www.perezhilton.com and www.tmz.com

www.perezhilton.com   www.tmz.com   Source: Hitwise

affluent urban group in the Claritas PRIZM segmentation, the 'Urban Uptown', characterized as college-educated people who frequent the arts, shop at exclusive retailers and drive luxury imported cars.

But the rich city dweller isn't the only consumer of celebrity gossip. If, for example, you're young and live in the suburbs or perhaps in a rural area, then TMZ might be more your style. TMZ, which according to the site stands for the 'thirty mile zone', also known as the studio zone, is here used to describe the epicentre of Hollywood, thirty miles surrounding the intersection of Beverly Boulevard and La Cienega. TMZ.com, which is a joint venture between Telepictures Productions (which produces shows such as *Ellen*, *Extra* and *The People's Court*) and America Online, has grown in step with Perez Hilton and jockeys for the position as the most visited celebrity blog site. PerezHilton.com and TMZ represent only the top of the celebrity blog food chain. As we travel farther down the trail, we find several celebrity websites that cater to specific audiences. If you are young and African American and live in a suburb or small city, you're more likely to visit Bossip.com than your rural counterpart is. If you live in the suburbs, along with TMZ, Hollywoodgossip.com may be more your style. If you're a hip urban professional, then Gawker is the site for you.

If Houran is right, that the increase in information we can access about celebrities exacerbates our feeling of knowing our favourites, then the influx of celebrity blogs means that more and more we're going to feel connected with our favourite celebrities, as we inch our way up the Celebrity Worship Scale.

FOR SOME, CELEBRITY HOLDS a more intense fascination than for others: What will she do next? Did she break up with him? Who will get the kids in the custody hearing? For most of us, consumers and marketers alike, celebrities at least wield the power to make us buy things. And no other celebrity in recent memory has fine-tuned that power as well as one woman has.

Whether it's a beauty product, a new book or even the latest-model Pontiac that you wish to promote, there is one afternoon talk show host who has the power to send your latest novel to the best-seller list, or your own TV show to the top of the ratings. Of course the most powerful celebrity endorsement is from Oprah Winfrey. Oprah herself has become an Internet phenomenon, holding the spot of most searched-on personality, with very brief exceptions, over the last three years.

That Internet power may extend beyond herself

and the products and services she endorses. For the first time since she became the most popular talk show host, Oprah has decided to back a presidential candidate. Prior to the primaries, Oprah appeared on *Larry King Live* to announce her support for Barack Obama. She had Obama on her show to discuss his platform, and as a result of his one appearance on the show visits to his site increased by an amazing 358 per cent in just one week. While we may not have an exact fix on viewers of *Oprah,* we can certainly get an idea of who constitutes an Oprah fan based on visits to her official site.

It's no surprise that Oprah visitors skew female, 72.8 per cent to be exact. Her Internet fans also skew slightly older, with 66.4 per cent of her visitors older than 35. And as far as regional spread, more than 35 per cent of Oprah's US visitors come from powerful voting states like California, Illinois, New York, Texas and Florida.

Oprah clearly has the power to make stars, from fitness gurus such as Bob Greene, to celebrity chefs like Rachael Ray, to pop psychologists like Dr Phil. Her power to expand beyond endorsements to affect public opinion, and even possibly political success, demonstrates the spell that she has over her vast audience. That spell might be the best example of Jim Houran's Celebrity Worship.

CHAPTER 6

What Are You Afraid Of?
and Other Telling Questions

What are you afraid of? It's a simple question, but your answer may depend on who is asking the question or the setting in which you're answering. Imagine you're talking with friends, maybe at the water cooler or over cocktails, when the topic of phobias comes up. How do you answer? Your response might be similar to the results of the National Comorbidity Survey,[15] a study of more than 8,000 respondents in the United States. In that study, those who agreed to be surveyed were asked about what they fear. From their answers, a list of the top nine groups of fears was developed:

1. Bugs, mice, snakes and bats
2. Heights
3. Water

4. Public transportation
5. Storms
6. Closed spaces
7. Tunnels and bridges
8. Crowds
9. Speaking in public

But how truthful are our statements about our fears, even if those statements are being made to the faceless voice of a telephone surveyor? Aren't we all, in some way, concerned about being judged for our fears, perceived as being weak or irrational?

Back at Hitwise in San Francisco, I sat on the floor of the office of one of my analysts, LeeAnn Prescott, throwing a NERF Ball in the air as we held an impromptu brainstorm session for posts that we could write to the blog. We were talking specifically about understanding society's collective conscience at any given moment by using search terms as the key to those thoughts. We considered separating out from the millions of unique searches in our database just those that contained the question 'why', as a way of understanding what people were seeking to understand, or 'how to', as the key to what people want to learn to do.

I can't remember which of us came up with the idea, but it was brilliant: to look for all search terms that contained the term 'fear of', as a way of understanding and potentially ranking our phobias, on the theory that some of us must be using search engines and the Web to try to understand our fears.

I walked over to LeeAnn's desk so that I could see the results. I was expecting to find a handful of terms, summarizing the most common fears. I was shocked when our system pulled 1,686 unique searches in a four-week period that contained the term 'fear of'. By quickly running through the list, I could see (1) the fears that we search on are not ranked in the same order as what appeared on the National Comorbidity Survey, and (2) our fears are unique, very specific and, in some cases, downright weird.

To create my list of the top phobias, the first task was to filter for non-phobic 'fear of' queries. 'Fear', after all, shows up in a variety of places, such as song lyrics; terms such as 'Fear Before the March of Flames', an experimental rock band from Aurora, Colorado; educational queries such as 'Definition of Fear'; and, of course, queries such as 'The Girls of Fear Factor'. After removing those terms that were clearly not phobia searches, we still found well over 1,000 unique fears to analyse.

Some terms were a little more difficult to classify as true phobias or mere curiosities. The second most searched-on term was 'fear of long words', which may have its origins in an ironic urban legend-inspired definition. When searching on the term we found several listings that claim the official Latin term to describe this fear is Hippopotomonstrosesquippedalio. (The actual Latin nomenclature for this fear is Sesquipedalophobia.) People searching on this fear are probably just amused by the fact that someone's come up with such a long word for it, rather than truly identifying with the fear. Interestingly, in searching for an explanation of this phenomenon, I found several websites that claimed to offer a cure for the fear of long words, including one on which a 'board-certified team specializes in helping individuals overcome fears, phobias & anxiety of all kinds, and is particularly focused on problems such as fear of long words'.[16] As I drilled further through these sites, however, it became clear that the site owners made liberal use of their word processor's search-and-replace functionality to create boilerplate text on every conceivable fear.

After all the filtering, we arrived at a list of the top searched-on fears for our sample. While the list isn't as direct as asking the question 'What are you afraid of?', it is a view of what fears we are trying to understand, typed into search engines, which, unlike our friends, relatives or therapists, are incapable of judging us.

Here are the top ten search terms from queries containing 'fear of':

1. Flying
2. Heights
3. Clowns (which may also refer to the movie *Fear of Clowns*)
4. Intimacy
5. Death
6. Rejection
7. People
8. Snakes
9. Success
10. Driving

One of the most noticeable differences between the list of searches on fears and the phobia list compiled by the National Comorbidity Survey is that there is only one social fear in the Comorbidity Survey top nine, the fear of speaking publicly, versus four in the 'fear of' searches: 'fear of intimacy', 'fear of rejection', 'fear of people' and 'fear of success'.

Psychologists group our fears into specific categories, distinguishing between social phobias, or those fears that involve our interactions with other people, and specific fears, which might include the fear of heights, spiders or public transport.

The big question then is why our search patterns on fear show significantly more social fears than what were found based on a survey. Estimates are that 15 million Americans, nearly 6.8 per cent of our populace over the age of 18, suffer from some form of social anxiety disorder.[17] Yet if these numbers are calculated on the basis of a survey, it's entirely possible that we're undercalculating those afflicted with social fears.

According to the National Institute of Mental Health, social phobia is defined as

> an anxiety disorder characterized by overwhelming anxiety and excessive self-consciousness in everyday social situations. Social phobia can be limited to only one type of situation – such as a fear of speaking in formal or informal situations, or eating or drinking in front of others – or, in its most severe form, may be so broad that a person experiences symptoms almost anytime they are around other people.[18]

If these social phobias are characterized by excessive self-consciousness, how would a person suffering from this fear respond to another individual conducting a survey about their fears? Wouldn't this be the perfect example of the cognitive dissonance issue that we discussed in the first chapter? But take the surveyor out of the equation and replace him or her with a non-judgmental tool that can access massive volumes of data, and this search data may hold the key to a more realistic gauge of our social fears.

I often bring search lists with me on trips and spend time poring over them to pass time during long flights. One of the most entertaining and enlightening lists to review was this list of 'fear of' searches. Within the top 100 searches, twenty are some form of social fear, but as you dive deeper into the list of 1,000-plus fear searches, the strongest recurring theme that presents itself is the battle between two types of social anxieties: the fear of commitment and the fear of being alone. Perhaps these searches don't rise to the level of clinical anxieties, but if search patterns are any indication these two opposing concerns are on the minds of many of us. Since we're not asking people directly what they are afraid of, there are some alternative explanations to the duelling fears of being alone and not being alone. One possibility is that searches like 'fear of intimacy' and 'fear of commitment' are actually the keystrokes of someone other than the fearful, such as the significant other in a troubled relationship.

Here are the top fifteen social 'fear of' searches:

1. Intimacy
2. Rejection

3. People
4. Success
5. Crowds
6. Failure
7. Sex
8. Commitment
9. Public speaking
10. Being alone
11. Love
12. Girls
13. Falling in love
14. Abandonment
15. Broken heart

There may be something more significant going on here. It's clear that social fears exist with more frequency in online searches than they appear in survey results. The difference in fear rankings may demonstrate that the survey responses are not truly reflecting what we're afraid of, but could our social fears also be exacerbated by the online experience itself? The mere fact that we choose to query a search engine versus talking to a friend, relative or health professional about our fears suggests that we find more comfort and privacy conversing with an algorithm on these matters than we would seeking help from one another. The problem becomes even greater as we delve into the very strange world of specific fears.

Specific phobias are entirely different, and truly demonstrate their unique nature. It's estimated that more than 18 million Americans over the age of 18 suffer from specific fears, more than 8.7 per cent of the US population. There are several categories of specific fears, from animal phobias (spiders, mice, bunny rabbits, which shows up towards the end of the list), to situational phobias (flying, tunnels, bridges), to environmental phobias (storms, heights), to 'other'. 'Other' is actually the most interesting group. As I wade through the 1,600 different 'fear of' queries, I'm struck by just how individual our fears are. While the social anxiety around being with someone and the anxiety around being alone make up the head of the query stream, the long list of specific phobias makes up the long tail or unique set of phobia searches.

Getting past more common fears, like the fear of flying, snakes and clowns, reveals some truly bizarre specific fears. Departing from the ontology developed by mental health professionals, I've developed my own grouping for these oddities of anxiety, ordered by popularity.

Fear of different body parts appears numerous times within the list, from what appears to be a not entirely uncommon fear of being 'touched on the neck' to fear of hair, teeth, skin, to the unique fears of elbows, feet, belly buttons, and more specifically the fear of 'belly button lint', which may be an extension of the more popular 'fear of dust'.

Our Internet searches also demonstrate the isolation of our society and our fear of other cultures, in fears that are hybrids between social and specific anxiety. Societal fear searches include queries such as 'fear of German things', 'fear of the French people', 'fear of Mexicans' and 'fear of Chinese culture'.

If I were to guess, I would say that fears of subjects of study are harboured by our school-aged children, with 'fear of maths' topping the list, followed by 'fear of biology' and 'fear of physics', and very specific fears such as the 'fear of the theory of relativity'. While I haven't previously thought of my apprehension around Einstein's theory, terms like 'time dilation' are certainly capable of causing me some unease.

Finally there are those fears that just defy categorization, such as the multiple occurrences of 'fear of fear', also known as phobophobia. Are some of us so debilitated by the possibility of acquiring a phobia that the fear of having a fear itself becomes our primary fear?

I struggle to figure out the basis for some of the odd fears that show up in the tail of the fear search queries. Common causes for specific phobias include a past traumatic experience or a learned response. While the fear of the number 13 is certainly understandable, given the superstition attached to that number, what could possibly be a past traumatic experience or learned response that would cause someone the 'fear of capital letters' or the 'fear of odd numbers'?

Given the vast collection of fears that we search for, in some ways it's comforting to know that so many of us suffer the fear of something, in some cases rational, in others seemingly irrational. One of the fears that didn't surface in the list is the fear of the unknown. That's interesting given that one of the most popular queries is a quest for 'how to' information. Perhaps since the explosion of information available on the Internet, the ratio of known to unknown has been in a rapid decline.

One extension of our fear searches, which confirms the potential of the Internet to become our confidant, is the nascent category of confessional websites. The online confession genre owes its genesis to Frank Warren, the author of the best-selling *PostSecret,* a collection of confessions submitted anonymously on postcards.

The concept, which started as an art project in 2004, led to the best-seller and eventually in 2005 to a website that featured Internet-submitted confessions.[19] In keeping with Internet tradition, several websites flourished by expanding on the idea of anonymous Web-based confessionals, such as the Experience Project, a confession website built around a social networking structure. Now not only could Web users submit their deepest, darkest secrets in anonymity, they could also get comments and responses from others who shared similar secrets.

Some confessional websites are devoted to specific predicaments or life stages. Truemomconfessions. com, for example, is an anonymous confession site devoted to the challenges of motherhood. The site's tagline is 'Motherhood is hard, admit it.' Perusing the site, you can find confessions such as 'I love my kids. I love being a mom and wiping butts and cooking 'kid-friendly' meals. I do not, however, necessarily like my kids today,' or 'There were days I wished to God that I stopped at one.' The founder of the site has also created other specific confessional sites, such as True Office Confessions, True Dad Confessions and True Bride Confessions.

When we look at the demographics of visitors to confessional websites, it's clear that at this time, just the beginning for online confessions, there is an Early Adopter (see Chapter 10) for this type of activity. Visitors to these sites tend to skew female (70 per cent), and live in affluent households in suburbia. Essentially, these websites are giving us a window into the online equivalent of Wisteria Lane.[20]

When we look at the collective activity on confessional websites, and what we choose to confess to search engines in the form of search queries, we have a pretty accurate collection of what weighs on our minds. While the Internet may cause us to withdraw from one another, the anonymity it affords us may, like the screen in a Catholic confessional, allow us the safety to admit things we wouldn't normally discuss with anyone else. This insight into the human condition isn't limited to what scares us or what we feel the need to confess. The increase in 'how to' queries provides another treasure trove of online data, telling us what we want to learn.

JUST THIS LAST YEAR I was faced with a fear, the fear of failing at a very specific task. I had just got off the phone with the managing editor at TIME.com, the online component of the magazine. Having read my blog posts on Internet data and talked with a colleague, Josh, the editor, wanted to know if I was interested in writing a weekly column. Was I ever! But wait, there was one glaring problem: I was at best an amateur writer, had never taken a journalism class; I was clearly not a writer by trade, and I had never written a column. *TIME,* one of the best-known and prominent periodicals in the United States, wanted to know if I was interested in writing a column; to say I was intimidated would be an understatement. Right after hanging up the phone with Josh, having told him that I was very interested, I instinctively typed the Google URL into my browser, and without even thinking, I placed my cursor in the empty search box and typed 'how to write a magazine column'.

Search engines have gone beyond serving the simple purpose of finding information or navigating to a website. Increasingly engines such as Google, Yahoo! Search and the other 1,000-odd search sites are serving as a source of knowledge and learning. Sitting around viewing the 'fear of' queries, the analyst team and I brainstormed for other interesting phrases to study. When we investigated the idea of 'how to' queries, we were astonished by the volume that this phrase represented. 'How to' queries represented nearly 3 per cent of all search queries in the United States, making it the most commonly searched question, and for that matter, phrase, entered into search engines. 'How to' searches also have seasonal patterns that coincide with the school calendar, with a peak that always occurs during the summer months, and then a subsequent decrease during the winter holiday and Easter break. And while 3 per cent may not sound like a large volume of searches, considering the hundreds of millions of queries that pass through search-engine servers each day, 3 per cent is a shockingly high number.

While I really do love analysing search lists and looking for patterns of behaviour, when I saw before me a list of the more than 130,000 'how to' searches the Hitwise system had captured in a four-week period, the task seemed insurmountable.

I started at the top. The number one 'how to' query, holding that position consistently over the last

Breadth of Searches on "How to"

——— "how to"   Source: Hitwise

two years, was 'how to tie a tie'. This one data point seemed odd. Of all the questions, things we'd like to know how to do, is tying a tie really on top of our list? My first question was: Is this a US phenomenon? In contrast to the United States, a quick check of our UK database put 'how to tie a tie' in the number 51 position. In Australia, 'how to tie a tie' was closer to US data, below 'how to vote' and 'how to write a résumé'.

I'm often asked at search conferences if there are differences in how Internet users from other countries search. There most definitely are. Sometimes they are as simple as differences in vernacular. For example, in the United States we are more likely to search for airline 'tickets', while in the UK airline 'flights' are more prevalent. Sometimes search data highlights differences in culture. Take the necktie. How do we explain the discrepancy between a number 1 US ranking and a number 51 ranking in the UK? My hypothesis is that since most schoolchildren in the United Kingdom wear ties as part of their school uniform, tying a proper tie becomes second nature, with no need of instruction, while in the United States neckwear for men has become a special-occasion skill set, one that may need a refresher. In fact if we chart the pattern of different 'how to tie a tie' queries over time, we find that they surge during the summer months, presumably for wedding season.

Things get interesting after neckwear. It appears that the most popular 'how to' searches are executed by sexually curious teens (only a guess based on the language and subject matter), with queries such as 'how to kiss', 'how to have sex' and 'how to make out'. Reviewing these hormone-charged searches, I'm wondering what teenagers did before the Internet. In my youth, to the best of my recollection, we fumbled through the mysteries of getting along with the opposite sex, too embarrassed to pose these sensitive questions to friends or, God forbid, family. In contrast, today's teenagers, through search engines, approach the Internet as a giant how-to manual. Going beyond the top twenty to the top 100 terms, it appears that teen boys are more likely to execute the most common 'how to' sex queries, given the high volume of 'how to find a girlfriend', 'how to flirt with girls' and more specific anatomical questions about females.

Has the Internet levelled the playing field between men and women? Among their female friends women are far more likely to share information on sexual experiences. Men are far less likely to do so with their male friends, but with shared experiences available on the Internet, are men and women now equally informed? The addition of the Internet as a resource for teens to answer questions regarding the opposite sex and sexual relations is causing a shift in the balance of knowledge between teen girls and boys. Based again on anonymity and the lack of embarrassment that a non-judgemental search engine provides, the balance of knowledge between the sexes may have equalized.

Figuring out how to do something via our computers is becoming an increasingly popular activity. 'How to' queries are on the rise. Since the beginning of 2007 they have risen more than 17.5 per cent. Here are the top ten 'How to' searches in the United States for the four weeks ending 21 December 2007:

1. How to tie a tie
2. How to have sex
3. How to kiss
4. How to lose weight
5. How to write a résumé
6. How to levitate
7. How to draw
8. How to get pregnant
9. How to make out
10. How to make a video

When you look at these terms, one thing that

becomes very clear, beyond teen sexual angst, is just how, like our fears, our instructional dilemmas have become fractionalized. To make sense of the vast list of more than 130,000 different searches, I grouped the top 1,000 'how to' searches into categories.

The most prevalent type of 'how to' queries are those general-knowledge questions that seek how to accomplish a specific task, which include our number 1, 'how to tie a tie', as well as 'how to make a movie', 'how to solve Rubik's cube' and so on. 'How to draw' figures prominently in this class of queries, with specific interest in drawing Japanese anime characters being the most popular. Combined, general-knowledge questions accounted for more than 57 per cent of the top 1,000 queries.

The next most common how-tos were of a sexual nature. Given the graphic nature of this set, I'll leave the list to your imagination. There were 173 of these queries out of our total of 1,000, or 17.3 per cent.

'How to' searches also reveal our aspirations. Comprising 12 per cent of the instructional searches were questions geared towards self-improvement: how to 'lose weight', 'gain weight', 'make money' and, for those truly in search of instant gratification, 'make money fast'. On the darker side, more than 9.5 per cent of the searches were for illicit or illegal activities, with marijuana use figuring high on the list (how to 'grow marijuana', 'grow pot', 'grow weed'), but also some very concerning questions: 'how to commit suicide', 'how to make meth', even 'how to make a bomb'. We apparently feel comfortable enough with our computers and the Internet to query just about anything. By the way, 'how to write a book' is in position number 62.

SEARCH ENGINES ARE GREAT resources for finding all kinds of information, from directions to finding a hard-to-locate computer part, book or long-lost friend, and even the long tail of information created by consumer-generated content. As we've just discussed, we are turning to search engines to understand our fears and to find out how to accomplish tasks, but sometimes our questions are even more basic. Sometimes we just want to know why.

By examining the patterns of search questions containing the term 'why' (which constitute more than 0.5 per cent of all Internet queries), we see that they show a strong seasonal pattern that correlates with the school year, reaching their peak during spring and autumn months, and dropping as much as 60 per cent during the summer and the week between Christmas and New Year. It's a good guess that a fair portion of our questioners are school-aged children. In fact some of the most popular 'why' queries seem likely to be generated from a school project. Questions pertaining to a holiday are likely to be posed near the holiday itself. For example, in November some of the most popular 'why' searches include 'Why do we celebrate Veterans Day?' and 'Why do we celebrate Thanksgiving?' Pulling 'why' questions during any other month of the year will also result in questions about the closest holidays.

It appears as though some students are showing educational fatigue, with questions like 'Why should

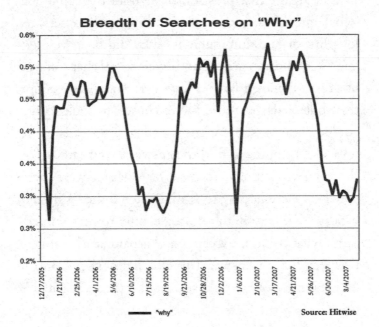

Breadth of Searches on "Why"

Source: Hitwise

I go to college?' and 'Why is college required?' After these basic questions, the general questions that you might expect to hear from an inquisitive child ensue: 'Why is the sky blue?' has been the top 'why' query for two years running (save the month that Britney Spears shaved her head, which led to intense 'why' scrutiny).

Sifting through more than 20,000 'why' questions from just a four-week period, as I get deeper into the list I see that questions depart from simple school project queries and become more complex, and sometimes moving, searches for meaning.

One theme that persists throughout the top 1,000 'why' questions is our relationships with others. A long line of questions such as 'Why did he leave me?' and 'Why didn't she say good-bye?' reveal that some of us are so troubled by our interpersonal relationships that, out of desperation, we've chosen to look to the computer servers, algorithms and indexes that make up a search engine to find the answer to our failures or the failures of others. To discover what answers these searchers were hoping to find, I entered the 'Why did he leave me?' search into Google, only to find numerous advice column excerpts and a paid search advertisement for an answer through hypnosis, 'Control Men Hypnotically – These secrets can open a man's heart.'

Farther down the list, beyond the educational queries, beyond the questions like 'Why do cats purr?', the questions become much deeper, more introspective and more philosophical. We question why things happen, our beliefs and our existence.

Religious queries play a central role in these introspective searches. Religious searches, however, are very different by denomination. The majority of Catholic 'why' searches, for example, seek to understand some of the customs and practices of the religion, such as 'Why do Catholics pray to Mary?', 'Why do Catholics pray the Rosary?' or 'Why do Catholics use holy water?'

Searches around Christianity in general reveal a concern about hatred, both in terms of why Christians hate, such as 'Why do Christians hate atheists?', as well as the flip side, 'Why are Christians hated?' 'Why' searches about Muslims contain a few hate-related queries like 'Why do Muslims hate the West?', but the majority of Muslim searches, like Catholic searches, seek to understand religious practices, such as 'Why can't Muslims eat pork?' and 'Why do Muslim women wear a hijab?'

The 'why' of Judaism stands out from the rest; there are barely any searches about the practices of Judaism. The majority of searches on the religion (and 'why' searches with Judaism or Jew within the query are the most popular searches of any religious denomination) deal with the Holocaust and the persecution of the Jews, with searches such as 'Why did Hitler kill the Jews?', 'Why were the Nazis so mean to the Jews?' and 'Why did Hitler hate the Jews?'

When we broaden the scope of the 'why' searches to just those that contain 'God', the struggle with the concept of religion reveals itself. There in various forms is an unmistakable theme, which is: If there is a superior being, then why, as Harold Kushner wrote in his seminal work, do 'bad things happen to good people'? The question takes many forms, from 'Why did God take him away?' to 'Why did God do this to me?' to the sceptical viewpoint of 'Why do people think God takes people?'

Questioning, as we do, everything from our deepest, darkest fears, no matter how irrational, to our faith and existence, we've made it clear that search engines have gone beyond being merely a tool to help us find information. Search engines, despite their limitations, have for some of us become a teacher, a confidant, a willing listener to our confessions.

For all the talk of how the Internet has enabled superior communication between us, it appears in some circumstances to actually reveal our insecurity, and in other cases, with its anonymity and its inability to judge, to provide us a way to avoid posing the most difficult questions or admitting our shortcomings face to face with our friends and relatives. And that leads to my question: Isn't this technology, which has so much potential to bring us together as a society by improving our communication, in some cases actually isolating us? If we continue on the path of relying more on technology to help us answer the basic questions about why we fear things, how to get things done and how to relate to other individuals, we will continue to drift farther apart. But one thing is certain: As we turn to search engines to answer our deepest questions, we'll continue to learn more about ourselves.

CHAPTER 7

Web Who.0

Defining Web 2.0 is a challenge for anyone who has attempted it. I co-authored a paper on the subject with the Pew Internet Group in 2006. The Web 2.0 concept arrived in my inbox in the form of an email from a friend urging me to watch an amateur clip on Google's video search service. Clicking through on the link launched a video of two Chinese students from art school in Guangzhou, China, lip-synching to the Backstreet Boys' 'I Want It That Way'. The combination of exaggerated facial expressions, synchronized movements and a stoic figure in the background made for a very funny video.

I found myself laughing uncontrollably at the antics of these two students half a world away. At the same time, I felt compelled to send the link to several of my friends that same day. Before long, the two students, known on the Internet as the Back Dorm Boys, Wei Wei (also known as the small one) and Huang Yi Ziu (the big one), had garnered more than 1 million views of the webcam video. From a simple lip-synched song, the two students went on to gain online fame, eventually signing as spokesmen for Motorola in China. The viral spread of content is not a concept new to Web 2.0. Viral marketing was the buzz term for the early 1.0 version of the Web. What changed was that, rather than circulating content created by content publishers, such as portals or the online versions of newspapers and magazines, in May 2005 we began circulating content created in dorm rooms, on webcams, in basements and home offices. A select number of Internet users had become the content creators.

I've never received so much hate mail/comments as when I attempted to put a stake in the ground on what was and was not considered a Web 2.0 site. According to the comments that I received, my big transgression was calling MySpace a social network and therefore a Web 2.0 property. I'm not sure why that definition raised so much ire on the part of the readers. It is apparent, though, from the responses, as well as from hisses from the crowd when I mention the term 'Web 2.0', that it is a term that is thrown around as a buzzword of the day, with little thought to definition.

While I stick by my original definition that 'Web 2.0' refers to those sites that allow users to generate their own content and share that content among other users, it may be more helpful to highlight the difference between pre-2.0 sites (we'll refer to them as Web 1.0) and their new network-enabled 2.0 versions.

During the first Internet bubble one of the most popular sites in the educational category was Encarta, originally a CD-ROM-based version of the traditional Funk & Wagnalls multi-volume hardbound set. Microsoft released the hybrid CD-ROM- and Web-based encyclopedia in 1995.[21] By the year 2000 almost all of the traditional encyclopedias had an online version, but it followed the traditional publishing model: articles written by professionals and edited by professional editors.

In January 2001 Jimmy Wales founded the 2.0 counterpart to Encarta, the social encyclopedia Wikipedia.[22] For Wales's new version of the encyclopedia, the traditional publisher/author/editor model was out the window. When Wikipedia launched, it was a blank canvas, where anyone, in anonymity, could create an entry on any topic. While at first the reaction to Wales's model was scepticism, posed primarily as the question 'Why would anyone want to spend their time writing an encyclopedia that provided no monetary incentive to do so?', the rapid growth of Wikipedia proved the sceptics wrong.

Not only did Wikipedia grow, it thrived, quickly surpassing its traditional 1.0 competitors. If we compare Encarta to Wikipedia, Encarta's premium edition has more than 68,000 articles on a variety of topics. Wikipedia, as of 2007, has more than 7.5 million articles written by more than 5 million registered editors, and new articles appearing on the site at a rate of 1,700 per day.[23] In the beginning of 2005 Encarta and Wikipedia were about the same size in market share of vis-

Market Share of Visits to www.encarta.com and www.wikipedia.org

www.encarta.com   www.wikipedia.org   Source: Hitwise

its. By the end of 2007 Wikipedia's share was more than forty-five times the size of Encarta's.

Web 2.0 versions of 1.0 sites show up in other areas, such as photo sharing. Pre-2005, computer users were flocking to sites like ofoto.com, ingenious sites that allowed you to upload your photos to a central server, then request prints or email your online photo album to friends. But up in Vancouver, British Columbia, Ludicorp, the maker of an MMOG, or massively multiplayer online game, called *Game Neverending*, stumbled upon a new application. One of the company's programmers had created a tool that allowed you to save a photo or screen shot while playing a game and then upload that picture to a website. The features later incorporated into Flickr that differentiated it from existing photo-sharing sites were the ability to open viewership of your photo to anyone who happened to be on the website and, more important, the ability to tag a photo, or add a text-based description that would allow anyone to search for and find your picture. As an example, if I were in Paris and took a picture of the Eiffel Tower, uploaded my picture to Flickr and assigned a tag to the photo, then anyone searching on 'Eiffel Tower' would find my picture along with 152,000 other pictures of the same landmark.[24]

This simple change, allowing everyone access to everyone else's photos, along with the idea to make photos (and later videos through YouTube and bookmarked sites through del.icio.us, to name a few) searchable through 'tagging', created a snowball effect similar to what enabled Wikipedia to surpass Encarta and other encyclopedias.

November 2005 was an inflection point in the adoption of Web 2.0. It was the month that YouTube, in the span of only a few weeks, surpassed more traditional video search sites like Google Video and Yahoo! Video to become the most popular video site on the Web. The world's content creators, such as magazine and newspaper publishers, television executives and a host of others, began to wonder if this new version of the Internet, which enabled consumers to generate and share any form of content, would endanger their own businesses. But was it reasonable to expect everyone to jump into this trend of content creation and sharing? Before we answer that question, we have to take a quick detour to Paris at the turn of the last century.

THE REPLACEMENT OF TRADITIONAL media with blogging and content generated by participants in Web 2.0 sites may herald the death of the Pareto

Principle, at least in regard to who produces and consumes information in today's world. In the late 1800s a French/Italian economist, Vilfredo Pareto, a leader of the Lausanne School, observed that in Italy 80 per cent of the country's income went to 20 per cent of the population, and also observed that 80 per cent of the country's property was owned by 20 per cent of its citizens. It wasn't until the 1900s that an industrial engineer at Western Electric by the name of Joseph Juran applied Pareto's observations to business, to develop what he called the Pareto Principle, or the law of the 'vital few', a hat-tip to Pareto's original observation.

The 80/20 rule's most popular application is the observation that 80 per cent of a company's revenues are generated by 20 per cent of its clients, but the rule has also been observed in countless other business situations, such as time management (spend time on the 20 per cent of tasks that are responsible for 80 per cent of your outcome) and quality control (fix the 20 per cent of problems that result in 80 per cent of defects).

With the distribution of content through the Internet, in the form of digital song downloads, blogs and user-created photo and video segments, the 80/20 rule may have become a relic of the bricks-and-mortar economy. As Chris Anderson noted in his *Wired* magazine article[25] and later in his book *The Long Tail*, when thinking about how distribution of content has changed in the Internet economy, it's easy, when asked about the sales of music online, for example, to want to apply the 80/20 rule. 'We've been trained to think that way,' Anderson says. 'The 80/20 rule is all around us.' He presents the example of Robbie Vann-Adib in his article. Robbie is the CEO of Ecast, a digital jukebox company. When asked what percentage of the top 10,000 titles in any online media store will sell or rent at least once per month, Vann-Adib's answer isn't what the 80/20 rule would have us believe (20 per cent according to Juran's concept); it's 99 per cent.

Jakob Nielsen, commonly referred to as the father of online usability and author of several books on the subject, addressed the topic in his online newsletter *Alertbox*.[26] Mr Nielsen noticed that in large online communities and social networks there is a division among visitors. There are users who actively contribute and there are those Nielsen refers to as 'lurkers'. He labelled this phenomenon 'participation inequality' and identified the breakdown of online visitors to social sites in a 1-9-90 spread, versus Juran's 80/20 distribution. According to Jakob Nielsen, 90 per cent of online users are 'lurkers', or users who visit online communities but don't contribute; 9 per cent contribute from time to time; and only 1 per cent of online users are active contributors.

Nielsen goes on to note that in terms of blogs, the inequality of active participation is even worse, possibly approaching less than 0.1 per cent of Internet users. It's ironic that the concept of consumer-generated media, portrayed in the media as a democratizing force that empowers consumers to participate in the conversation versus just being spoken to, is really limited to a very small fraction of all Internet visitors.

In the interest of finding out more about Nielsen's participation inequality, we examined the participatory elements of three Web 2.0 sites: YouTube, Flickr and Wikipedia. To accomplish this we used one of the custom tools we have at our disposal: looking through the changes that occur when a visitor to one of these sites participates by uploading content (for YouTube, uploading a video; for Flickr, uploading a picture; and for Wikipedia, editing an entry). Once we identified the URL for each of these activities, we allowed the system to gather data for four weeks. By doing this, we had the opportunity to quantify user participation in three major Web 2.0 sites, but what was far more exciting was the opportunity to learn the 'who' of Web 2.0, or the difference between a static viewer (or lurker), an occasional participator and a power contributor.

Our first month's worth of data confirmed Jakob Nielsen's article. In the case of YouTube, of all the visits to the site from US Internet visitors, only 0.16 per cent were identified as uploads of video content. For the photo-upload site Flickr, 0.18 per cent of visits to the site were marked as those where someone uploaded a photo; the remaining visits were simply people viewing the vast content of uploaded photos. The data from Wikipedia showed something quite different. More than 3.5 per cent of visits to Wikipedia were identified as someone entering text after clicking the 'edit this text' button. So what accounts for the percentage difference in participation when we compare Wikipedia with YouTube and Flickr?

The most plausible explanation is that there is a sliding scale implicit in the 1-9-90 rule that is dependent on the complexity of participating in a particular application. The effort required to upload a home-made video to YouTube is quite different from the simplicity of clicking on a tab in Wikipedia and editing an entry. Based on our observations of this data over several months, we've come up with our own 1-9-90 rule, a variation on Nielsen's original. Based on our data, we found that less than 1 per cent of all Internet visits to Web 2.0 sites are attributable to consumer-generated media (such as a video uploaded to YouTube); 9 per cent (this actually can vary between 3 and 9 per cent based on complexity) are visits where users interact with consumer-created content through either editing an entry or adding comments; and 90 per cent remain lurker visits, where Internet users are passively viewing content without interacting at all.

One common question that I get is whether the 1-9-90 rule is a function of technical complexity. Stated another way: As it gets easier to create and upload content, will the 1 per cent of actual contributors increase, or is the 1 per cent a function of desire to upload and create content, regardless of complexity? To answer that question, we could track the percentages for each group over time. If we make the assumption that creating and uploading content becomes easier over time, and if the percentages hold steady over the same time, then it's likely that the percentages are a function of desire to contribute, which, based on an anecdotal set of six months of data, appears to be the case. Another way of addressing this is to answer the 'who' question of Web 2.0.

When we look at visits versus participation for two sites, YouTube and Wikipedia, we can see that there are clear differences among who participates, based on demographics like age, gender and socio-economic class. For Wikipedia visitors, there is no difference in gender, with both site visitors and those who are editing entries split evenly between male and female. There is a significant age difference, however. With viewers, there is a large contingent of 18–24-year-olds, making up almost 25 per cent of these visits. When we narrow our field to only those visitors who have edited a Wikipedia entry, the 18–24-year-old group drops to 17 per cent. At the same time, entry editors skew towards older visitors, with 41 per cent over the age of 45; for visitors overall, those over 45 are just 33 per cent. The data appears to be telling us that Wikipedia demographics are a case of the old teaching the young. What's more interesting and puzzling is the difference in socio-economic class. Middle-class Wikipedia users from the suburbs, smaller towns and rural areas are more likely to edit entries than are site visitors overall, including the urban middle class.

Among YouTube users, there is a clear gender difference between visitors and participants (uploading videos). For visitors, there's a relatively even 51/48 per cent male/female split, while uploading a video shows a clear difference between men (58 per cent) and women (42 per cent). When we look at the age split for the two types of user, at first it's surprising to see that the predominant group for uploading is the 45–54-year-olds. To understand this particular age spike, it's important to know the time frame in which the data was pulled and to factor in one of the intricacies of online data measurement. This particular stat comes from a spring 2007 set of data. During spring break (March specifically), as well as summer and winter break, we see spikes in this particular age group for YouTube; these are most probably attributable to the college-aged children of the account holder visiting home while on holiday.

The other interesting difference between visitors and uploaders to YouTube is where they live. When we compare passive visitors to those who actively participate by putting videos online, we see that visitors from small towns and rural areas are more likely to upload than their urban or suburban counterparts. Could it be that rural users have the luxury of extra time on their hands or fewer distractions?

WHAT DO YOU DO with 1,000 friends? Not a question that I expected to ask myself as I wrote this book, but there I was with just over 1,000 friends displayed in my Facebook profile. As I watched the rise of MySpace from 2003, and then Facebook's surge during 2005–6, I analysed the surges as a dispassionate outside observer. I could almost understand some of the hype that the media was spinning regarding the paradigm shift that social networks were causing. At the same time I had a sense that I just wasn't getting it. I needed to know first-hand what was so disruptive about a technology that it would cause Microsoft to invest $580 million for only a 1 per cent stake in Facebook. I decided that I needed to immerse myself in this new trend.

I created my own Facebook profile in a matter of minutes and began the task of inviting friends. After going through every online address book and mining the hallways of Facebook for long-lost friends, I reached a point of exhausting my list of potential friends, a paltry 124. I began to understand the competitive fire that builds in the belly of a serial Facebooker. I didn't believe that I was getting the real experience. My Facebook friends were mostly in my age group or my industry, and I had the sense that most of us didn't have a clue as to why we were on the site, or what to do now that we had got there and needed more friends, specifically some that might understand this new phenomenon.

In one of my weekly columns for *TIME,* I decided to write about the addictive nature of Facebook. At the end of my column, after my signature line, I convinced my editor to add a line stating that I had only 124 friends on Facebook, and that if

Market Share of Visits to Email Services and Social Networking Categories

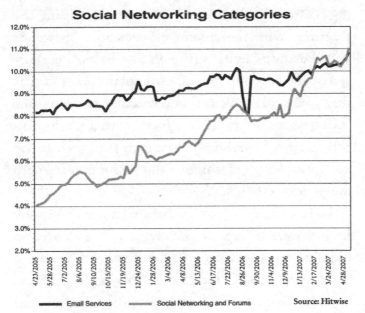

anyone happened to be in the neighbourhood, to drop by and send me a friend request. Within one week I had upped my account to 850 friends, and within a month I was over 1,000, among them friends from around the globe, including Europe, Asia and Africa. I also had added a significant number of prime Facebook users – university students.

In the process of getting to know one another, my new friends and I exchanged messages (all within the Facebook service). A common thread that ran through most of my conversations was that

social networks, Facebook specifically, were changing the way the younger generation was using the
Internet. With the advent of networks of friends
and the status update (the ability to post a short
statement to your profile to explain what it was
that you were doing at that particular moment, like
'Bill is at work,' or 'Bill is busy with a work project'), users of Facebook are able to scan their entire
network of friends quickly and communicate with
much more efficiency.

In fact the data corroborates what my Facebook
friends were telling me. If we look at the chart on
page 181 of the market share of visits to Web-based
email services (sites like Yahoo! Mail, Hotmail and
Gmail), which until recently was the most popular
category of websites based on market share of visits,
we find that as of summer 2007, for the first time,
visits to social networks had surpassed email.

One of my new friends, Lauren, an ex-pat living
in Switzerland, provides an example of how life has
changed from her parents' day of communicating by
'snail mail' to the amount of connectiveness that social networks have brought to relationships among
her peers:

> Something I find fascinating about our FB/
> MySpace generation, is its intimate touch on

our romantic relationships. Never before has
there been a time when we could know so
much about a person we are involved with. We
know when they are online, who they are talking
to, what their favorite *Family Guy* quote is, if
they choose to poke someone else instead of
us. Many of my male and female friends are
professed FB stalkers [of] their close friends
and significant others. FB hacking and message snooping are petty offenses in the name
of 'well, I just want to know who they are talking
with.' My parents waited weeks to hear from
each other by letter when my father was
deployed; I know the moment my boyfriend
steps in front of his computer.

All of this information flooding into our lives
begs the question: Will we ever get to the point that
we have too much information?

BEFORE I HAD SET foot in the place, even before I had
boarded the plane to London, I knew everything I
needed to know about my hotel. I knew that my room
would have two levels, that there would be five steps
down from a landing by the room door to a sunken
suite. I knew that the bathroom would have heated

floors, and that when I stepped into the bathroom I would be standing on green marble tiles, the shower would be on the right and I would find full-size Molton Brown bath products. I knew the name and physical description of each of the front desk staff and knew that Veronica was the person to ask about restaurants; she knew all of the best Indian restaurants in the Knightsbridge area. When breakfast was served the next morning in the basement dining area, I knew the best time to arrive to get a table and I knew that, even though I was in London, not Paris, I should skip the typical English scone and head for the croissants. (Although she never made an appearance in the dining room, the chef made the baked goods in-house and she was originally from Paris.)

I gathered all of this information in a matter of minutes by visiting just one site, TripAdvisor.com. The site, which began in 2000, was later acquired by the online travel company Expedia in 2004. On its site, TripAdvisor, which specializes in hotels, claims to have more than 10 million reviews of more than 200,000 hotels in 28,000 cities. They even have 825,000 user-uploaded photos covering 53,000 hotels.

How influential is TripAdvisor to the online travel industry? Of the 2,700 destination sites in the Hitwise Travel category, TripAdvisor has maintained the number one or two position consistently over the last three years, getting more visits than any major hotel chain and any destination or resort. At a travel conference in Barbados (travel companies always pick the best locations for their industry conferences), I had the chance to talk in between conference sessions with an executive of a five-star hotel chain. In my speech I had mentioned TripAdvisor and how it had empowered consumers with information flow like we had never before experienced. 'You know,' he said, 'in the past I could rely on my brand to keep my hotel full [his hotel brand had international recognition that was synonymous with five-star quality], but these days my brand doesn't mean as much, my five-star AAA rating isn't very useful. I find I'm spending most of my time keeping up with how many bubbles I have on TripAdvisor.'[27]

What this executive had noticed, and what almost all hotel chains have realized since, was that the transition of the Web from a static medium to a place where consumers could post their own content in the form of reviews and pictures was having a dramatic effect on their industry. In the world of Travel 1.0, or first-generation travel websites that allowed users to compare prices for hotels across multiple agencies, consumers had the best shot of finding the lowest possible price for their trip accommodations. In essence, traditional online travel sites removed a huge inefficiency in the marketplace. Consumers, now able to search on the properties they were interested in, were no longer at the mercy of a travel agency or hotel registration desk to find the best price.

But in this second shift, the Travel category's version of Web 2.0, the addition of voluminous numbers of hotel reviews has essentially commoditized hotel rooms. If, before I book a room at a hotel, I know what everyone else is paying (I search using Hotels.com or a travel search engine like Kayak or Mobissimo) and I know what I'm getting for my money – the quality of service, the condition of the room, even down to the brand of bath products – as a consumer I'm armed with perfect information.

The term 'perfect information' is a concept that is used in game theory and economics to describe the state where two parties are playing a game that has sequential moves with each party knowing exactly what moves have been made up to the current moment (chess and draughts are excellent examples of games of perfect information). D. W. MacKenzie, an economics professor at the State University of New York at Plattsburgh, has found a very accessible way of explaining the concept of perfect information: the movie *Groundhog Day*.[28] In the movie, the main character, played by Bill Murray, relives the same day of the year, Groundhog Day, multiple times in

succession. At first Murray makes some bad decisions, mainly involving a potential love interest, but
as he continues to live the day over and over again he
knows what is going to happen, so based on his now
perfect information he is empowered to make decisions with assurance of the final outcome.

Travellers who visit the TripAdvisor site, or other
consumer-generated review sites, might find themselves approaching a state similar to Bill Murray's.
Living vicariously through tens, maybe hundreds, of
previous hotel guests' stays, they can begin to build a
knowledge base of exactly what they might experience. Combine research into the best price you can
get for a hotel with knowledge of the experience, and
the consumer can now make a decision that is independent of a hotel's brand. But there's one problem:
Perfect information is a theory; the true state of perfect information is unattainable in real life.

While there may be several impediments to reaching true perfect information, two issues predominate
when examining the issue in the light of consumer-
generated reviews. First, perfect information relies on
consumers' motives and their ability to provide accurate information. In order to foster participation,
almost all sites give users the option of providing information in complete anonymity. While some may
be more truthful with a completely obscured identity

(feeling more comfortable providing a brutally honest critique of a local restaurant if they don't have to fear reprisals should they dine there in the future), others will use anonymity as a licence to provide reviews that distort truths. As Peter Steiner immortalized in his famous *New Yorker* cartoon that depicted two dogs talking while one was on the computer, 'On the Internet, nobody knows you're a dog.'[29]

In talking with players in the travel and hospitality industry, we learned that there are two suspected motivations behind two different kinds of false reviews: the shill review and the personal attack. Many property owners are suspicious that other property owners themselves are using anonymity to pump up the ratings of their own hotel or restaurant. On the other side, some property owners complain that their good name can be smeared by a single reviewer who attacks them with a textual vendetta for something that may have been explainable as a simple misunderstanding. And in the worst case, owners claim that some other owners deliberately attempt to lower a competitor's rating by anonymously posting erroneous negative reviews.

Another, more benign problem is the matter of viewpoint. Consumer reviewers of products and services bring their own individual perspectives to the reviews that they upload to sites like TripAdvisor or newcomer Yelp.com. And as Internet users incorporate more consumer reviews versus professional reviews into their choices of products and services, the matter of viewpoint can become critical.

Yelp was started in the summer of 2004 by friends Jeremy Stoppelman and Russell Simmons. The site bills itself as a 'fun way to find, review and talk about things that are great in your world'. As on the TripAdvisor site, Yelp content is based on user reviews, but with Yelp, users review everything, from restaurants and bars to dry cleaners, dentists and doctors, even Yelp itself. A busy restaurant in a metropolitan area like San Francisco can amass hundreds and sometimes thousands of reviews, with Yelpers assigning a one-to-five ranking to their review along with a narrative of their experience.

If we look at the psychographics of visitors to Yelp.com, the problem of viewpoint becomes very clear. Using Experian's MOSAIC segmentation to examine Yelp, we find that the largest group that visits the site is part of the H group or 'Young Contemporaries'. This group is made up primarily of Millennials who range in age from 18 to 24. According to MOSAIC, they tend to be 'big culture buffs who like to see plays, movies, comics and bands'. Since, as a group, they were 'raised on technology, they are very Internet savvy, spending their leisure time online to chat, job search, send instant messages, bid in auctions and frequent internet dating web sites'.

While this group is probably the most likely to visit and post reviews, the group members might be somewhat different from another key MOSAIC group that likes to peruse the site: group A, called 'Affluent Suburbia'. Members of this group tend to be households occupied by baby boomers and their older children. They generally hold managerial and executive positions, with primary interests that include money management, travel and gourmet dining.

Imagine how a review for the same restaurant might differ if it was coming from a 20-year-old Young Contemporary versus a 48-year-old Affluent Suburbanite. An act as simple as clearing plates from the table might lead to wildly divergent experiences and resulting reviews, each stemming from a different viewpoint.

Restaurateurs are widely divergent on the proper staff response to diners who finish their plates at different times from other members of their party. Traditional restaurant etiquette states that it is only proper to remove all the plates when everyone has finished a course. If our typical Affluent Suburbanite had never experienced anything different, he would probably interpret individual plates being cleared as diners finished as the server trying to rush the table. On the other hand, a diner from the Young Contemporaries might not be as knowledgeable about old-school restaurant etiquette. After finishing his meal well in advance of his dining partners, he may have placed his knife and fork in the centre of the plate to signal that he was finished, expecting a server to remove his plate promptly. Our Young Contemporary might be silently fuming while texting or checking his BlackBerry under the table, wondering why a restaurant with such reviews has, in his opinion, such lax service.

Upon returning home, each of our diners might log onto a restaurant review site like Yelp, one commenting on the excellent service – five star – while the other comments that he can't believe the restaurant has received such high reviews with such indifferent service.

While Web 2.0 is still considered a buzzword, surprisingly the industry is already discussing Web 3.0. Web 2.0 has made incredible strides just in the last two years, taking us from a static medium to one that encourages all of us to participate, but the movement has also created unique challenges, primarily how to deal with the massive amount of content that is available. If I could place my vote for Web 3.0, the need I see created by the consumer-generated content coming from

Web 2.0 is a method to filter all of that information for similarity of viewpoint, reputation and accuracy. Until that occurs, all of this content faces the prospect of becoming a collection of noise that we may not bother to rely on in the future.

If I had to identify an industry that has been hit the hardest by the Internet, I would pick the newspaper industry. From a revenue perspective, newspapers have lost subscription income to free news on the Net. Classified revenue has taken a significant impact from the likes of eBay and online classifieds such as Craigslist; even obituaries have been hit by online memorial alternatives.

The biggest impact on the newspaper business model has been in the timeliness of reading news on a daily basis versus having a continual updating stream of news available, again for free, on the Internet. By the time my newspaper hits my front door in the morning, I've already read about the earthquake in Asia, the latest political scandal in Washington, and the local news from my town, San Mateo. Even editorials and columns have been consumed before my morning cereal. And the problem doesn't stop there.

Along with traditional online news outlets, we are turning to alternative online sources to consume our daily news, reading political blogs rather than political coverage in the paper, celebrity blogs like Perez-

Hilton.com versus the paper's Lifestyle section. What's an industry to do when all of its value is in the process of being replaced by a resource that is virtually free to the consumer? As most newspapers have found, the answer lies in embracing that model, offering as much timely content as possible on the Net, and changing their business model to rely increasingly on Internet ad revenue versus subscription fees and print advertising.

Some papers have gone further, deciding to embrace the concepts of Web 2.0 and opening the floodgates to consumer participation. For some, that strategy has begun to backfire.

I found myself in the offices of a client, a major newspaper, meeting with their executive team. Our data had indicated that since they had incorporated user-generated content into their newspaper website, they had lost almost half of their online readership, dropping dramatically in our rankings. It turned out that this newspaper, believing in the hype of user participation, had decided to dramatically alter their website, making it much more '2.0'. What the executive team had not factored into their decision was Jakob Nielsen's 1-9-90 rule, applying instead the commonly accepted Pareto principle of 80-20.

To make matters worse, the psychographic segments that made up the online readership for this paper weren't the segments that were likely to contribute user-generated content. In fact the core readership segments were the steadfast consumers of news in its traditional format, the paper that landed at their door each morning.

The urge to rush into the world of Web 2.0 isn't specific to the newspaper industry. I've seen similar scenarios play out in online retail, travel and dating services to name a few. There are also examples where companies have successfully embraced consumer-generated media and their readers or customers have followed wholeheartedly. These fortunate companies either understood the who of Web 2.0 or were lucky enough to have the right mix of Early Adopter segments to embrace the change.

2 WHAT'S POSSIBLE WITH WHAT WE KNOW

CHAPTER 8

Data Rocks and the Television–Internet Connection

A s I sat on the panel awaiting my turn to speak, I cursed myself for being such a procrastinator. I didn't have an opening for my twelve-minute speech on the 'Search Engine Landscape' and had only finished my slides that morning, a few minutes before the session began. The opening was the most important part. The ballroom at the New York Hilton was filled to capacity. The New York Search Engine Strategies Conference, a gathering of search-engine experts and online professionals, had become one of the most popular conferences of the year. As one of the most lucrative sectors on the Internet, search engines carried a buzz that felt like the familiar Internet bubble. As the talks began, people outnumbered seats, forcing latecomers to sit in the aisles and on the floor in front of the stage to hear what three data-centric analysts had to say and watch data-heavy PowerPoint slides on what was happening with the search-engine industry.

As the first speaker was wrapping up his speech, it hit me. Since it was my first time speaking at this event, I had expected that my panel would draw an audience similar in size to the pharmacy conference in Philadelphia where I had spoken the previous week, in a bowling-alley-like room with a scant thirty to forty conference attendees interested in hearing about data. Yet here I was, unexpectedly sitting in front of a standing- (and sitting-) room-only crowd of 300–400, about to discuss the same data.

As a kid growing up in South Florida, I loved data. While the other kids in my neighbourhood found amusement in games and sports in the Florida sunshine, I was enthralled with finding patterns in the numbers. I was even more interested in the absence of all patterns, numbers like pi, whose digits stretched into infinity without once repeating a pattern. The difference was that when I was a kid data was decidedly uncool, whereas today, if attendance at this conference was any indication, data was very cool – or maybe I was in the wrong room.

As I walked up to the podium to begin my presentation, I decided that I would start with an

AA-style admission: 'I'm Bill Tancer, and I love data.' There was some nervous laughter in the room. (I thought maybe some were planning to make a quick exit and head to another session.) I went with the flow and talked about my childhood and how my love of data then might have caused me to appear to be uncool, but now data appeared to have become hot. There were a few giggles in the crowd as I moved on to my charts. But then a funny thing happened at the end of my talk. Some people came up to chat about my slides, and as one man handed me his card he leaned in and, almost under his breath, said, 'Hey, I love data, too.' The 'I love data' introduction became a standard opening for my speeches that year. With each speech, the 'data lovers' became more vocal, culminating in my return to the same search conference a year later, when data lovers began writing 'I love data' on the business cards they handed me, or 'Data is the new black.' As Internet statistics spread outside of the IT office and into the marketing department, mostly in the form of site-centric studies (the usage statistics available about your own website), more people ventured into the world of data.

A year later, as I prepared my speech for the upcoming Search Engine Strategies Conference (once again the morning of), I thought about the previous year's slides. I had presented statistics showing the standing of the major search engines and some information on demographics, and introduced the up-and-coming categories of vertical search (search engines that specialized in specific categories, such as shopping-comparison engines like Shopzilla and Shopping. com, local search and travel search). But this year I would tap into one of the richest sets of Internet data, the search data itself. In any given four-week period we had several million unique search terms in our database, all arranged in order of the volume of searches on each term. As John Battelle described it in his book *The Search*, I had access to 'the database of intentions', a collection of what our sample of Internet users were searching on each day. Battelle describes it this way: 'This information represents, in aggregate form, a place holder for the intentions of humankind – a massive database of desires, needs, wants, and likes that can be discovered, subpoenaed, archived, tracked, and exploited to all sorts of ends.'

Let's start at the head of the query stream, looking at the top ten searches typed into the fifty-five most popular search engines in the United States (of more than 4.6 million searches) for the week of 15 December 2007:

1. Myspace

2. Ebay
3. Myspace.com
4. Craigslist
5. Youtube
6. www.myspace.com
7. Walmart
8. Mapquest
9. Yahoo
10. Facebook

The first thing that strikes us about the list is that one brand, MySpace, the hit social network, is represented in three of the top ten spots. Back in the early days of MySpace, we noticed its rise in the search-term list. At the time we believed that what Internet users typed into a search engine, among other things, was a great measure of brand equity. We postulated that the quick rise in MySpace searches foretold the social network's popularity. In fact, by the look of this last set of data, MySpace is the strongest brand on the Internet today.

One thing that's noticeably *missing* from the top ten is any generic search terms. Where are the searches for 'cars' or 'lyrics' or 'music'? The answer to that question is twofold. One thing that has become very noticeable is the prevalence of domain ('myspace.com') and navigational ('www.myspace. com') searches. I've had many online experts, analysts with leading online research firms, look at our lists of top search terms, and they've viewed these navigational terms with scepticism. 'There must be something wrong with your data,' I recall one analyst saying. But having viewed the raw search logs from one of the major search engines, I know that searchers do in fact type domain names, and sometimes full Web addresses, into their favourite engine as search terms. Why would anyone do that?

There are two theories, and my guess is that both of them are right. First, some Internet users may type the full Web address into a search engine due to ignorance of the difference between the URL bar (the address bar in your Web browser where you type in the full URL) and a search box, reflecting a lack of sophistication in browsing the Web.

The other possibility is that brand and domain searches are the product of very astute Web browsers. More advanced Web users have probably reset their default start page either to their favourite social network or to a search engine like Google. If Google is the page where the browser starts each time the application opens, it's actually easier to type a brand ('myspace') or domain name ('myspace.com') in the search box than it is to move your mouse up to the URL bar in the browser.

Over time we have seen an increase in the sophistication of the searcher. The number of words per query has been steadily increasing over the last four years. This shows that Internet users are becoming more comfortable with asking more of their search engines. While four years ago some users would have been content to search on such a broad term as 'car', over time those searchers have realized that they can refine their search to 'Volvo S80', or a more specific '2007 Volvo S80', or to an even more sophisticated local search such as 'New Volvo S80 94402'. Just three years ago only 14 per cent of all searches had three or more words per search. In 2007 that number increased to 23 per cent of all searches.

One car search in particular, for the Pontiac Solstice, demonstrated the power of Internet data to measure our response to television. In April 2005 I was watching the latest episode of *The Apprentice*, spread out on my couch, laptop nearby. I noticed that this show had reached new heights (or lows, depending on your perspective) in advertising for its sponsors. In this particular episode, the contestants on the show, up-and-coming entrepreneurs broken into two teams, were competing on a project to design the best brochure for the new Pontiac Solstice. During the segment, Pontiac aired a sixty-second commercial that provided viewers with a Web address, www.pontiac.com/solstice, to register for the right to buy one of the first 1,000 special edition cars. I quickly made a note to check out search data when it updated on Monday of the following week.

That next week, a chart of searches on 'Pontiac Solstice' proved just how effective GM's marketing campaign was. Searches on the new car had quadrupled from the previous week. This simple chart demonstrated the potential for measuring the effectiveness of a well-done product placement in driving consumers to the Web and even to take the next step in purchasing a car.[30] In the traditional world of market research, to understand if a particular promotion was effective, you could measure sales after the promo-

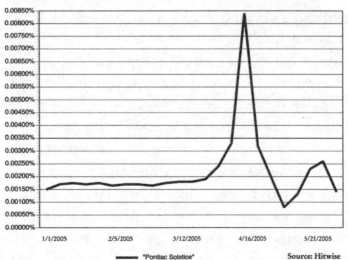

Volume of Searches on "Pontiac Solstice"

Source: Hitwise

tion, but you might have trouble relating those sales back to a particular advertisement; or in the least reliable scenario you could conduct focus-group studies or surveys of consumers to find out if they recalled the advertisement and what their opinions of it were. What I found most intriguing was that by monitoring a very large sample of Internet users I could produce a quicker and more accurate measure of the effectiveness of a particular advertisement, using an increase in search-term data as a proxy for the lift a promotion gave a particular brand.

I could also measure the brand associations that the *Apprentice* segment created, by looking at all of our search terms that contained the word 'Solstice' and then sorting those terms by volume of searches. Here are the top ten search terms containing 'Pontiac Solstice' for the four weeks ending 23 April 2005:

1. Pontiac Solstice
2. 2006 Pontiac Solstice
3. 'Pontiac Solstice'
4. 2006 Pontiac Solstice Pictures
5. 2005 Pontiac Solstice
6. Pontiac Solstice the Apprentice
7. Solstice Pontiac
8. Pontiac Solstice Reviews

9. New Pontiac Solstice
10. Pontiac Solstice Apprentice

Not only did the *Apprentice* segment succeed in raising the volume of searches on the new Pontiac car, now Internet users were associating the new car's brand with the reality show. This one product placement opened up a new world of potential analytics. We went back through that season of *The Apprentice* to measure the effectiveness of other placements, from Burger King to Dove and others. All other placements paled in comparison to the Pontiac Solstice, due in part to the effectiveness of an Internet call to action featured on the show. In analysing other product placements during multiple seasons of *The Apprentice,* I noticed that those that provided an Internet call to action tended to drive greater Web traffic.

But GM wasn't finished for the year. I did a double take in astonishment later that year, sitting again on the living-room couch, when I saw the first Google-Pontiac television commercial. The commercial, which was panned by online marketers as an example of traditional marketers misunderstanding the minefield that is search marketing, featured the new Pontiac G6. At the end of the commercial, the voice-over didn't give an AOL keyword, so popular in the nineties, or even a Web address. Instead the voice-over said something that caused me to choke on the water I was drinking at the time. The slick commercial with sexy images of new G6 design features transitioned to a screen shot of a Google search page, while the voice-over urged viewers not to 'take our word for it. Google "Pontiac" to discover for yourself how design can make a difference.'

As a market researcher involved in the search-engine sector since the mid-nineties, I immediately recognized just how bold and risky GM's commercial was. When you direct people to search for 'Pontiac' on Google, as a marketer you have limited control over what appears on the next page, something we call the SERP, or search engine result page.

There are two key portions of the SERP that Pontiac would have to take charge of in order not to lose control of where television viewers ended up after following the television commercial's directions.

The first area, which includes a shaded portion at the top of the page, along with another portion that runs down the right side of the page, is labelled 'sponsored listings' and is where advertisers can purchase an ad that is displayed if an Internet searcher searches on a specific word or phrase. (The advertiser pays for the ad only if the searcher clicks on the advertiser's paid listing.)

The second area that Pontiac marketers would have to be concerned about, even more so given the difficulty of controlling the results, was what is referred to as the main body of the search results. Search results displayed front and centre on the Google result page are not paid for; rather, this display of various listings is controlled by Google's algorithm, a computer process that sorts through the billions of Web pages indexed by the search engine to find just those pages that are most relevant to the user's search. Since the mid-nineties, a whole industry of search-engine optimizers, or SEOs, had sprung up, with the specialty of increasing a company's chances of being displayed in the main body of search results, for their brand and for searches relevant to their products and services.[31]

Fewer than a few seconds had elapsed before I opened my laptop, jumped to the Google page and searched on 'Pontiac' just as I was directed. I had to see if GM's gamble would pay off. In the number one paid position (at the top of the page, above any other paid listing) was an advertisement for Pontiac, but right below that was a listing for a site with the address www.mx5nocomparison.com, a site apparently developed by Mazda specifically for the Google

Pontiac commercial. The main search results weren't much better. While Pontiac did succeed in grabbing the number one, or top, organic result in the main search results, below that were listings for the Pontiac, Michigan, Bar & Grill, maps of Pontiac, Michigan, and various other unrelated results.

While most in the online marketing field sniggered at GM's decision to throw themselves on the mercy of the Google algorithm and paid search results, I was ecstatic. Not only could I examine the effectiveness of television ads in driving brand, but now, with such a direct call to action in a national television ad campaign, I could see the end result when traffic hit Google searching for 'Pontiac'.

The first question that popped into my head was: How well do people take direction? Did they just Google 'Pontiac', or were they inclined to search for something more specific, like the 'Pontiac G6' that was the subject of the television spot? Or, even more interesting, when you urge people to Google 'Pontiac', do they consider Google to be a verb, or a combination of noun and verb? In other words did everyone search 'Pontiac' on Google or did some search on Yahoo! or MSN Search?

First, we analysed where people went from Google once they had searched on 'Pontiac'. We knew from experience that on average a brand such as Pontiac should receive roughly 85–90 per cent of the search traffic on its brand. (The remaining 10–15 per cent might go to review sites, forums, image searches, etc.)

When the commercial premiered, Pontiac's share of search traffic on their own term dropped to 66 per cent, with Mazda capturing more than 4 per cent of searches on 'Pontiac'. But what did happen was that viewers of the commercial apparently followed directions. More users 'Googled' Pontiac than searched for the term on Yahoo! Search or MSN Search, and Internet users did Google just 'Pontiac', even though the commercial was for the Pontiac G6, which experienced no increase in searches during the commercial's run.

While these insights had big potential in the advertising and brand market research field, what was truly exciting was that unlike the traditional market researcher, who designs a survey, recruits people to answer it and then analyses the answers, I was looking at a data set that had so many answers embedded in it, all I had to do was ask the right questions.

As I found more examples like Google-Pontiac and began sharing them with audiences at my different presentations, enthusiasm for the potential of this massive database continued to grow. And conference attendees became more vocal in *their* love for data.

Walking between sessions, I'd get routine drive-by data confessions from other attendees: 'I've been fascinated by data since I was young.'

My obsession with finding more connections between our offline world and online behaviour continued to expand, and television commercials were the most fertile ground for finding these connections, so I quickly became a 'wired' couch potato, much to my wife's displeasure, looking up anything that might shed more light on how television media translated into online search behaviour.

To break out from the pattern of finding online components of offline behaviour, I started examining the data from the other direction. Rather than waiting for a story or commercial and then looking for corroborating search behaviour, I started with the search behaviour itself. By looking at the top search terms overall, as well as search terms to specific categories of sites, like political or news sites, or even down to specific site searches, I could find interesting stories right in the search data – and that is what led me to the Golden Spruce.

One of the most interesting sites to track for search-term lists is Wikipedia. The communal encyclopedia, which we discussed in more detail in Chapter 7, has a collection of more than 7.5 million user-generated articles on almost every conceivable subject. Wikipedia also has a reputation for being one of the first search listings in the main body of the search results on Google.

I've always been fascinated by the search terms that send traffic to this behemoth of information, because of what those search results represent: the topics that we'd like to know more about. The top ten search terms sending traffic to Wikipedia are surprisingly predictable, with some mainstay searches as well as those more occasional terms that vary due to time of year, news stories or the latest celebrity gossip. Here are the top ten search terms sending traffic to Wikipedia in the four weeks ending 4 February 2006, excluding Wikipedia-branded terms.

1. Encyclopedia
2. Hurricane Katrina
3. Sex positions
4. Chinese New Year
5. Sudoku
6. Rosa Parks
7. French Revolution
8. Alexander the Great
9. Benjamin Franklin
10. Martin Luther King Jr.

Just by looking at the list above I could tell you the month and year that it was pulled from. 'Hurricane Katrina' as a search term gives us some reference to the year. Since the deadly storm made landfall in August 2005, this list must have been pulled after that date. 'Chinese New Year', which is based on the lunar calendar, varies between January and February each year, but the presence of 'Rosa Parks' and 'Martin Luther King Jr.' so high on the overall list is a good indication that this is a February list, as February is Black History Month. Put it all together, and you know the list was pulled in the first February after Katrina's August landfall. Therefore this was a February 2006 list of terms.

Because it is my favourite search-term report, I make it a habit to pull the Wikipedia list once a month and review what seasonal topics are top-of-mind for the month. The June 2006 list presented a mystery that once again showed how connected our online media is to traditional media. For June 2006 the seventh most popular term driving traffic to Wikipedia was 'golden spruce'.

The top ten Wikipedia search-term list rarely surprises me. The appearance of a name or event that I didn't recognize could only mean that I had missed a major news story or online trend. To discover what I'd missed, I fired up the Google home page and quickly searched on the term. The search results identified a book by author John Vaillant called *The Golden Spruce: A True Story of Myth, Madness and Greed,* a non-fiction account of a 300-year-old Sitka Golden Spruce and the ecoterrorist who cut it down to make a point. The book had been published in May 2005, a full year earlier, so book publicity was unlikely to be the cause of the prominent search result.

Farther down the search results there was a link to NPR's coverage of the book, but again the timing was completely off. This scenario just wasn't making any sense. During that same period the search term 'golden spruce' was trumping terms such as 'Harry Potter' and 'David Beckham', perennial Wikipedia search favourites.

But there was an even more bizarre aspect to the data. Google, at the time, was responsible for sending more than 60 per cent of the online encyclopedia's traffic, yet when I pulled the top search terms on Google for the same time frame, 'golden spruce' was nowhere to be found. One of the tools that we have access to is a view into what sites are visited after a search on a term and, from the other direction, what search engine a site is visited from. Google was sending only 4 per cent of the 'golden spruce' traffic to Wikipedia. The number one search engine for the term was Ask.com, with 95 per cent of the searches. (During that time frame Ask.com was responsible for just 3.6 per cent of all Internet searches.)

Another clue was what other sites were receiving traffic on the term. Wikipedia was number two. The number one destination for 'golden spruce' was NBC .com, the online component of the television network. An extensive search of that site, however, revealed no reference to the mysterious tree. I was fortunate enough to have on hand the head of global infrastructure for Hitwise, Richard Crane. Richard was equally perplexed by the golden spruce, but by tracing the actual full Web address that was clicked on, he discovered that the golden spruce traffic from Ask to NBC was specifically going to an online streaming video.

In the summer of 2006 NBC premiered their new reality television series *Treasure Hunters,* which sent teams of three on a hunt across the United States, using clues presented on the show. In an innovative tie-in, NBC, along with its sponsor Genworth Financial, ran an online contest where, with a unique set of online clues, Internet users could play along for a chance to win $100,000. One of the first clues, which was presented only in a streaming online video, urged the treasure hunter to 'go to the land of the Golden Spruce'. Displayed on the screen along with the clue was the icon for the search engine Ask. com, which explained why so many Internet users chose to execute their search on the Ask.com engine.

The potential to win cash in online contests and sweepstakes is one of the strongest incentives to move Internet users from remote control to computer keyboard, strong enough in this case to create one of the top search terms of more than 160,000 sending traffic to the world's largest encyclopedia.

CHAPTER 9

Women Wrestlers and Arbitraging Financial Markets

One of the first rules of FOO camp is that you don't talk about FOO camp. The annual gathering that began in Sebastopol, California, was the genesis of the un-conference movement. Rather than having a set schedule of speakers and sessions, an un-conference leaves the creation of the agenda to the attendees, usually to be decided at the beginning of the conference. FOO, in the case of this gathering, refers to the friends of O'Reilly, Tim O'Reilly, founder of the premier publisher of computer books in the world.

On the way up to the event on a warm day in June, I stopped by the local outdoor equipment shop to pick up a new tent. This particular conference was *very much* an un-conference, with most attendees putting up tents in the grassy area around the apple orchards that surround the O'Reilly campus. My spatial skills don't translate very well to tent assembly, or tent location for that matter. I paid little attention to the bright orange circle painted in the grass; I assumed at the time that the circle represented some sort of boundary. With no tents within the circle, I made the correct assumption that my new Sierra Designs three-person tent (tent designers must be Lilliputian in stature) would fit just fine. I didn't notice the bright 'H' painted in the middle of the circle.

The 'H' in this case stood for Larry Page's helicopter, which proved to be a worthy adversary for my poorly erected tent. In a new location, I was surrounded by Internet brain power: Jimmy Wales, founder of Wikipedia, was in a two-man directly in front of my tent; Mitch Kapor, founder of Lotus Development Corporation, and Shel Kaplan, employee No.1 for Amazon.com, happened by to help me get assembled in my more sheltered new location.

As I wandered around the grounds, feeling like a new kid at camp (which was entirely the case), I struck up a conversation with another neophyte. Michael Simonsen had heard of my company and knew of our data. Michael's firm, Altos Research, is in the business of harvesting real estate information from the Internet and using that data to arbitrage information about the real estate market. 'Arbitrage' is the key term here. As

we began discussing the synergies between our different data sets, I told Michael I had been thinking about
the opportunities to predict markets based on Internet usage. Michael enlightened me to the fact that we
weren't actually predicting anything with our data;
rather, we were each just very fortunate to have a data
set that allowed us to see what was already happening
in a market – be it housing, employment, consumer
spending – before anyone else had the opportunity to
see what was happening.

It seems like a simple distinction, but there's
quite a difference between the art, often perceived
as voodoo, of predictions versus straightforward
arbitrage. Predictions involve assumptions, calculations and, above all, substantial room for error, depending on the precision of your underlying
assumptions and calculations. Data arbitrage, on
the other hand, is simply taking advantage of the
time differential between when people do something on the Internet (such as search for a home for
sale, or place their residence up for sale) and when a
financial indicator such as existing home sales
would show that activity. The gap between the two
can be a matter of days or weeks or even months.
The greater the better.

I first began to practise what I now consider data
arbitrage in a Dallas hotel room in 2006.

I was in town for a travel conference, speaking about how travel agencies, airlines and hotel chains can use competitive intelligence data to compete more effectively online. Sometimes I find that I can't work in silence; I need a small distraction, so I turn on the television and surf the channels to find something that I don't have to pay total attention to. That night it was the first part of the finale for ABC's *Dancing with the Stars* (season 2) – perfect.

As I got back to preparing my presentation for the following morning, working on a slide that demonstrated the importance of search to the travel category, a thought occurred to me. I stopped everything that I was doing. Looking up as the final dancers completed their turn, I heard the show's host talk about how to vote for your favourite couple. This reality show is based on a format where each week the judges score the dancers on a scale of one to ten. The audience then has the opportunity to vote via a telephone number, by text or by visiting the official website for the show and casting a vote. While I had no insight into how the judges would vote, I realized that the show was essentially a popularity contest between the dancers. If I'd been measuring popularity based on how often Internet users searched on products or services or even people, then the search data that I had access to should also correlate to audience call-in.[32]

Doing a quick check of my hypothesis, I charted the three finalists from the prior season: soap opera star Kelly Monaco, actor John O'Hurley and boy band singer Joey McIntyre. While it was a single anecdotal data point, the chart certainly looked compelling.

Kelly had nearly thirty times the volume of Joey McIntyre, who placed third in the series. I felt a rush of adrenaline as I put aside the travel conference presentation and prepared to chart the current season's finale.

The finale for season two was a face-off between women's wrestling diva Stacy Keibler, deemed by judge Bruno Tonioli to be a 'weapon of mass seduc-

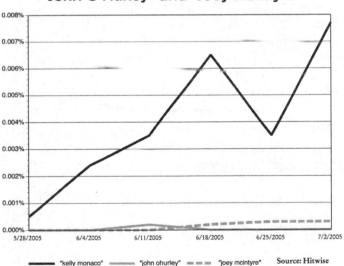

Volume of Searches on "Kelly Monaco", "John O'Hurley" and "Joey McIntyre"

"kelly monaco"   "john ohurley"   "joey mcintyre"   Source: Hitwise

tion'; former NFL wide receiver Jerry Rice; and former member of the boy band 98 Degrees Drew Lachey. If my hypothesis held, then I should be able to predict the outcome of the current season in advance of the announcement of the final results. One of the advantages to our interface is the instant gratification of seeing a chart within seconds of typing in the parameters. I could chart back two years any category of website, or even an individual term, as I was doing here.

Within a few seconds I had my new chart showing the volume of searches on season 2 contestants.

It was as compelling as the previous season's chart.

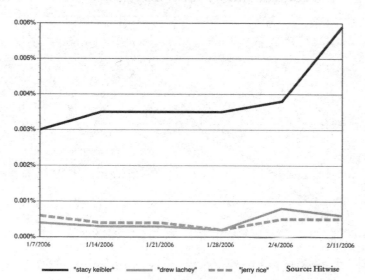

Volume of Searches on "Stacy Keibler", "Drew Lachey" and "Jerry Rice"

Woman wrestler Stacy Keibler, in terms of search volume, was the runaway favourite, with almost ten times the volume as nearest contestant Drew Lachey. While my presentation the next morning had nothing to do with reality television or the entertainment industry, I decided to throw the chart in anyway. Sure enough, judging by the crowd's reaction to the last slide in my deck, I hadn't been the only one watching the *Dancing with the Stars* finale the night before. I was so confident in my prediction that I mailed the chart to the staff at Hitwise, demonstrating an exciting new use for our search-term data. All I had to do now was wait for the next evening, when the show's final results were going to be announced.

I was comforted when I saw the latest odds on the show's finale. Pinnacle Sports, an offshore betting site, was listing Keibler as the overwhelming favourite, with 1:2 odds. Perhaps they were seeing something similar to what I had seen the night before.

If you followed that season of *Dancing with the Stars,* you'll know that not only was I wrong, but my predictions were the opposite of the actual results. Stacy Keibler placed third, with Drew Lachey winning the season and Jerry Rice placing second. As I walked into the office the next morning, I was prepared for the ribbing from my colleagues, having made such a public prediction on anecdotal data only to have the results show the opposite. Oddly, though, I was looking forward to coming into the office that morning. I was fuelled with curiosity as to why my predictions were so off.

There were some obvious explanations that I had to rule out first. By judging popular opinion, I was accounting only for half of the contestants' score; the other half was supplied by the judges, whom I had no way of predicting (although I could study ballroom dance scoring to make an educated guess). There was also the issue that a phone voter might represent a different demographic than an Internet searcher; maybe there was no correlation between the two and my season one chart was just a lucky coincidence.

I was actually closer to the problem than I realized: The issue was with the demographics of who was searching on the finale contestants. Opening up the chart again, I wondered if there was any way of determining who was searching on Stacy, Drew and Jerry. First I wondered if there were clues in the way that Internet users searched for Stacy Keibler. Using a tool called a search-term suggestion report, I created a list of all of the search queries that contained the words 'Stacy Keibler'. For the four weeks ending the week of the finale, there were more than 400 different ways that Internet searchers were looking for Stacy Keibler online. Looking at the top ten terms, I immediately knew the problem. Almost all of the searches for Stacy Keibler were looking for pictures or photos of the long-legged wrestler turned dancer. To confirm my suspicions, I took the next step and traced where the majority of 'Stacy Keibler' searches ended. The number one site that Internet users visited after searching on Stacy was the Official Women of Wrestling site, www.owow.com. Once past the welcome screen, the next screen displayed a gallery of nude female wrestling pictures (Stacy Keibler was not among them). It's not a reach to guess that the site is not targeted by the typical *Dancing with the Stars* voter. A check of the site's demographics confirms that point. Visitors to OWOW.com are male (72 per cent) and under the age of thirty-four (52 per cent); in other words, an audience that wouldn't be caught dead phoning in a vote for Stacy Keibler to win a ballroom dancing show (but is happy to look at some provocative pictures of her).

This revelation led to the next generation of search analysis, using term volume. We realized that search terms can't be analysed in a vacuum, that in some cases there may be multiple reasons why an Internet searcher will search on a particular product, service or celebrity name. We jokingly refer to our new method for examining search intent as applying the SKCC, or Stacy Keibler Correction Coefficient.

Armed with our new insight into factoring search intent, we went on to correctly predict the winner of the British counterpart (and original edition) of *Dancing with the Stars,* named *Strictly Come Dancing,* as well as the winners of several other reality television shows. *American Idol* presented a more straightforward prediction challenge in that judges have no vote; results are determined solely by viewer call-in or text votes.

Predicting the winner for season five of *American Idol* appeared to be a no-brainer. 'Taylor Hicks' searches exceeded 'Katharine McPhee' searches even without considering a correction to McPhee's search-term volume based on searches for a wardrobe malfunction that she had prior to the finale. My wife smiled and shook her head as I posted my prediction to the Hitwise blog and then called a journalist who covered entertainment for *USA Today* to inform her of my prediction. 'I guess you've got a fifty-fifty chance,' she said. But I knew that, based on the search data, I had a greater chance of being correct. And I was.

I don't really look at our successful (and unsuccessful) attempts at naming the winners of reality shows as predictions. More accurately stated, as I discussed at FOO camp, we are arbitraging data. Search data, if analysed properly, gives us insight into what viewers might think of a particular performer before actual votes are tabulated. The reality television show examples were entertaining and a great learning experience in arbitraging data, but the exercise served its true purpose as proof of what was really possible with search-term data.

ONE OF MY ARBITRAGE exercises started back in my early days at the company. Having loosely grasped the concept, I was in search of opportunities where I might gain insight into a statistic that experienced a time lag. A CNBC broadcast announcing the weekly unemployment claims number released by the US Department of Labor was all it took. I needed to find a number that required time to collect and report, and which my near real-time reporting would allow me to arbitrage based on the time delay. The Department of Labor tabulates unemployment claims across the United States for each week, ending on Sunday. The report is issued on Thursday of the following week. Hitwise market-share data for visits to websites updates every afternoon from the previous day's data; search-term data updates every Monday from the previous week's data.

Clearly I had a time advantage over the Department of Labor, but what was the connection of online searches and site visits to unemployment claims?

Standing and waiting at the local state unemployment office to apply for unemployment is quickly becoming an obsolete practice as most states now allow applicants to complete their paperwork online. If I could find enough data on visits to state unemployment websites, I could combine them into a set that I could track as a group. Given that an increasing number of the unemployed are applying online, by tracking the ebb and flow to my custom group of sites, along with searches for 'unemployment', I could compile a statistic that should correlate with the weekly number released on Thursday.

If only life were that easy.

There were some complications, to say the least. I had data on twelve of the fifty state unemployment websites, and luckily they were the largest unemployment sites, giving me more than enough, but potentially skewed, data, undercounting the unemployed from less populous states. Then there was the issue of seasonal activity. The number released by the Department of Labor is a seasonally adjusted unemployment number. These seasonal adjustments are made to account for recurring movements of the workforce such as major holidays and school schedules. Of course, Internet visit

Visits to Unemployment Websites and Unemployment Claims

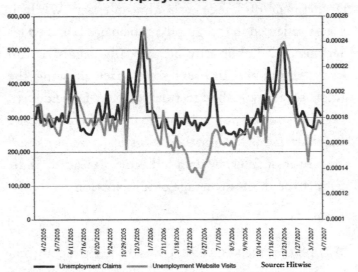

Unemployment Claims ——— Unemployment Website Visits   Source: Hitwise

and search data is not adjusted, and must either be compared with the unadjusted number, or the adjustments must be applied to the data.

On the other hand, Internet data of this sort experiences its own seasonal fluctuations, such as yearly application requirements and visits to unemployment websites to gather tax information. Once both of these issues were accounted for, the resulting data should, I thought, provide a leading indicator of the weekly unemployment claims number, or at least provide a view into the number's directional movement.

The match between the Internet statistic and the

actual unemployment claim number released by the Department of Labor was almost exact. While it wasn't reflected in the graph on the page 229, the Department of Labor number actually lagged a full week behind the Internet stat. After showing the graph to Hitwise hedge fund clients, I decided to look for an even more dramatic indicator. Again the search was on, for another statistic to demonstrate the power of Internet data to become a leading indicator through the arbitrage of information.

MAYBE IT WAS BECAUSE I was brought up in real estate (both my parents were real estate brokers) or that I had been through two stressful real estate transactions in California, and like the rest of the country I'd become obsessed with the value of my home. It only seemed natural that I tackle the real estate market next.

The number to match was that of existing home sales, a stat that is released monthly by the National Association of Realtors (NAR). In the Internet age, almost everyone considering buying a home at some point will go online and research the marketplace, visiting sites like REALTOR.com or a local real estate agent's site to access the consumer version of the multiple listing service. If this Internet research phase of purchasing a house is pervasive, then Internet data might be the key to predicting other indicators, like the NAR existing home sales number.

Like unemployment figures, the existing home sales number is a 'hard' number that takes time to compile; but unlike the unemployment number, it is reported only monthly, giving me a greater lead time. Gaining insight into existing home sales using search-term data is a much more complex problem than forecasting unemployment. I decided to forgo using visits to real estate sites as a predictor simply because those visit numbers can be influenced by online marketing programmes. In other words, if a real estate site decides to attract traffic by buying advertising space on a portal page like Yahoo! or MSN, it may entice users to the site when the user isn't necessarily in the frame of mind to purchase real estate, thus artificially inflating the number of visitors, so that it does not necessarily reflect market conditions. Search terms are a different matter.

While an Internet user's decision to go to a search engine and search for real estate information might be indirectly caused by online (or offline) advertising, search terms provide a more direct measure of user interest in buying or selling a home. I toyed with building a complex model based on a variety of different search terms, in the hope of finding a combination that would function as a leading indicator to home sales, and in the process I started comparing individual real estate terms with the NAR number. To find what terms I should be charting, I generated a list of the most common real estate terms. (We could determine which terms these were by tracking all of the search terms that sent traffic to the top 1,900 real estate sites in our Business–Real Estate category.)

I didn't get very far. The first term I charted, the most popular search term for the real estate category that week, was the term 'homes for sale'. The pattern of searches on the term appeared to be a great match for the ups and downs of existing home sales. Checks of other terms on the list did not even come close.

Still remembering the misfortune of my first reality television prediction, I took it slow with 'homes for sale'. At first I started with internal emails to some Hitwise staff, and then a post on the blog to announce my prediction. Word got out, and before I knew what was happening I was booked to appear on CNBC to discuss my prediction for the upcoming August 2006 existing home sales number. The prediction went as planned. During the CNBC taping, the anchor asked for my September prediction. Having prepared for this question in advance, I explained that for the Sep-

Volume of Searches for "Homes for Sale"

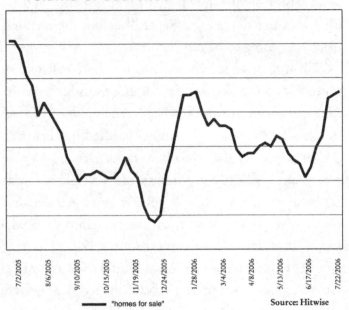

7/2/2005 · 8/6/2005 · 9/10/2005 · 10/15/2005 · 11/19/2005 · 12/24/2005 · 1/28/2006 · 3/4/2006 · 4/8/2006 · 5/13/2006 · 6/17/2006 · 7/22/2006

"homes for sale" Source: Hitwise

tember data we'd finally see a directional change in existing home sales. (They had been on a precipitous decline since spring. What I didn't anticipate was the next question, 'Would you be willing to come back on air with us when next month's numbers are announced?' She was asking me on the air, so there was really only one answer: 'Of course I would.')

The month that transpired between my on-air prediction and the day of reckoning was filled with anticipation. States, and individual counties as luck would have it, usually report their numbers in advance of the national number. I had an open spreadsheet on my laptop that I was updating multiple times per day as the September numbers rolled in. It was going to be close.

When the day finally arrived for the NAR to announce existing home sales for the month, I was in Manhattan on business. Matt Tatham, the Hitwise media relations manager, and I huddled in his office and prepared for the two obvious scenarios: (1) I was right, and here's my prediction for next month, and (2) I was wrong and here's why. It had been decided the day before that instead of heading into the main studio that day in Englewood Cliffs, New Jersey, I would be filmed from a remote studio in Manhattan. As we headed over to the CNBC office, I reviewed all of the economist predictions that had been rolling in over the previous week. The consensus was for more than a 2 per cent decline in existing home sales compared to the previous year.

To say that the room I was ushered into at CNBC's New York office was a remote studio would take a big stretch of the imagination – think broom cupboard. The cramped space was jammed with a television camera, a backdrop and a stool for me to sit on. The woman meeting me in the reception area, who showed me to my close quarters, handed me an earpiece and quickly left the room, closing the door behind her.

As I got situated, I heard Jane Wells's voice come

through the earpiece, with the strange sensation that she was actually in my head. Jane, who was producing the segment, could apparently see me via the camera in the room and asked me to do a quick sound check.

Eight minutes to the 'hit time'. (I was getting familiar with broadcast lingo; apparently this was the time that I would go live on the air.) Silence through the earpiece. With only a minute to go, Jane was in my ear again: 'The NAR just released the number; you were wrong.' My heart sank. 'What was the number, Jane?' I asked. 'A 0.5 per cent decline compared to the previous year.' Thinking quickly, I recalled that the mean economist prediction was for more than a 2.5 per cent decline. My prediction was for a change in direction. 'Jane, I was almost right!' was all I could think of. I don't know how they did it so quickly, but as I looked down to my lower right there was a monitor of the show on tape delay. As we went on the air, there was my name and title, and below that, in quotes, 'almost right'. Ouch.

During the taxi ride back, all I could think of was what I had missed in making the prediction. Had I not factored something into searches for 'homes for sale'? Over the last year the term had predicted every directional shift in existing home sales. If there was one law that superseded my predictions, it was Murphy's Law (if anything can go wrong, it will), but why now, and why this?

Remembering the lessons learned from the first *Dancing with the Stars* prediction, I didn't waste any time before checking out 'homes for sale' searches for the past month and any information I could gather about the intent behind the searches.

One thing we did know about the real estate market was that by the summer of 2007, in many markets, there was an impasse between buyers and sellers. Existing home sales continued to drop, but sellers had not lowered their home prices in response to the lack of buyer interest. At the same time buyers, perhaps sensing a pending drop in prices, refused to meet sellers at the current price levels.

As I rechecked the search terms driving traffic to the Real Estate category, something caught my eye that hadn't in previous weeks: There were several terms inching their way up the ranks that had to do with home values. Checking where Internet users were going after searching on 'homes for sale' revealed another surprise. Since I'd checked last, there had been a change in the top sites getting traffic on the term. Rather than national real estate chains and multiple listing services taking the top rankings, real estate voyeurism sites (sites that provide the amounts of recent transactions, as well as estimates for home values) were at the top.

So while the incidence of searches for 'homes for sale' was increasing, the change in destination site was indicating that perhaps, for the first time in the last two years, the search wasn't being executed by interested home buyers; it was a search from worried home owners, wanting to know what had sold in their area and whether their own home's value had dropped in the stagnating market. I'd been bitten again by the Stacy Keibler Correction Coefficient.

THESE RATHER RUDIMENTARY METHODS for creating a leading economic indicator were just the beginning of our journey in finding opportunities to arbitrage data based on Internet behaviour.

Over time, through the attempt to gain insight into a number of different real-world outcomes from Internet activity, it has become very clear that the data is always right, but pitfalls exist in how we interpret it, from gleaning insight from search terms to knowing the difference between search intent and actual behaviour.

Another maxim that I've learned over time is that the simpler the better when it comes to data arbitrage. Our clients in the financial sector, such as hedge funds, investment banks and financial research firms, have applied Internet behaviour data in the simplest form. In an extension of the unemployment data, I thought of a simple exercise. If a company sells goods exclusively online, and if in a given period of time they have not altered their average sales price or business model, then the market share of site visits that we record over a financial quarter should correlate tightly with the company's quarterly revenue. The stock price of any given company can depend a great deal on whether that company makes or misses its quarterly revenue expectations. Using those assumptions, I applied my simple model to online companies such as Amazon, Overstock and others. We had great success at directionally predicting company revenues. While the results were in no way definitive, any edge that a trader can get in guessing the market's direction on a specific issue can be an extremely valuable tool.

While the data itself can be the most effective predictor, filtering all that we know about a large sample of Internet users can produce broad results. As luck would have it, there are a few segments of the Internet population who act as bellwethers for the latest trends. In some trend predictions, it's best to start with a well-connected, tech-savvy individual, someone who would be voted most likely person on the block to adopt the latest technology – the Early Adopter.

CHAPTER 10

Finding the Early Adopters

Do you ever wonder how innovation spreads from an idea to mass adoption? For example, how did Google, which at its initial inception was named Backrub, ever unseat the established leaders in search at the time, companies like Yahoo! Search, MSN, Lycos and AltaVista? How did Google go from being a complete unknown to owning over 65 per cent of all US search traffic? With all of the business plans and recently funded ventures in Silicon Valley, how does that one idea – and ones like it, businesses like YouTube, MySpace and Facebook – find a way to rise above the rest and spread its influence at lightning speed to quickly become the market leader in its space? If only we had a way of knowing what might be the next great technology.

The study of idea diffusion, or how ideas or technological innovations spread through society, was on the mind of Harvard sociologist Bryce Ryan when he ventured out to an Iowa cornfield at 4 am on a summer day in 1939. Ryan, who must have seemed very out of place standing in the cornfield before the break of dawn, was conducting research on how an improvement to corn seed, a new hybrid variety, might spread throughout farms in two Iowa counties.

The new hybrid corn seed was a vast improvement over traditional seed, with the potential of increasing corn production by more than 20 per cent. Since there was no clear downside, common sense would dictate that farmers across the two counties that Ryan was studying would plant the new hybrid seed immediately. But according to Ryan's study, the adoption of the new seed was hardly an overnight affair; it took nearly twelve years for the new hybrid to become fully accepted at the farms that he studied. Why the delay?

When Ryan studied the problem, he noticed that there were key groups of farmers who adopted the new seed in advance of other farmers. In fact Ryan had identified several segments of farmers, each group appearing to rely on the previous segment's adoption before they made their decision to use the new seed. In studying the rural Iowa corn farmer,

Ryan had identified a process by which new products or technologies are adopted in society, and he had done this by recognizing the influence structure of personality types in social networks.

Everett Rogers, who studied the results of the Iowa hybrid corn seed as well as research around the adoption of other new technologies, from new antibiotics to mobile phones and VCRs, coined the phrase 'diffusion of innovations' in his book by the same title. When Rogers plotted the frequency of those who adopt technology by the time it takes them to adopt that technology, the resulting curve was bell-shaped. By examining the characteristics of technology adoption across this curve, and using standard deviations, Rogers identified five key segments on the adoption path of something new. To the far left of the curve were two crucial segments, the Innovators and the Early Adopters, who were followed by the Early Majority, the Late Majority and the Laggards.

The Innovators in Rogers's curve play a vital role in taking a new idea from outside the normal boundaries of a specific area and introducing it to the market, acting as gatekeepers for the flow of new ideas into a system or marketplace.[33] But while the Innovators might appear to be the target for a marketer's interest, it's the Early Adopters who have proven to be the catalyst by which a new product moves from being an exciting innovation to dominating the market by achieving mainstream adoption. According to Rogers, the Early Adopter 'more than any other category, has the highest degree of opinion leadership in most systems'.[34] Essentially, while the Innovator has the foresight to know what products and technology are going to help a certain marketplace, the Early Adopter has the eyes and ears of the subsequent adoption segments, and the power to influence what becomes a success in the marketplace.

Countless marketing texts and landmark works, like Geoffrey Moore's *Crossing the Chasm,* have been devoted to understanding the product adoption life cycle and the concept of marketing to the Early Adopter to give any product the best chance of moving to mainstream adoption, which ultimately leads to success in the marketplace.

There is one major challenge to the idea of Early Adopter marketing: How do you find members of that very valuable segment? Aren't their identities dependent on the type of product or service that you are seeking to market?

UNLIKE HYBRID CORN SEED, with its twelve-year-long adoption curve, the Internet, specifically the much-hyped Web 2.0 space, is prone to hyper-innovation. As we saw with the adoption of properties such as YouTube, a site can rise from being a relative unknown, still in its early phases of testing (referred to in development as the alpha or beta phase), to suddenly, within only a few weeks, overtaking the established players in a specific category and becoming the market leader.

As of the beginning of 2008, the video sharing site YouTube owns the online video space. Of the 470 different multimedia sites visited by US Internet

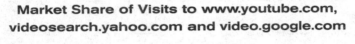

Market Share of Visits to www.youtube.com, videosearch.yahoo.com and video.google.com

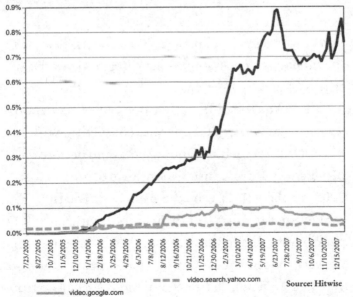

Market Share of Visits to www.youtube.com and videosearch.yahoo.com

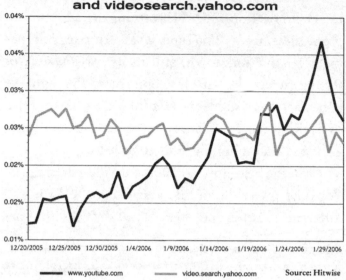

Source: Hitwise

users that we track at Hitwise, YouTube has held on to the number one position in that category over the last two years, with 51 per cent of all visits to those sites.

When YouTube officially came out of its beta release, at the end of 2005, it was competing with the likes of Internet giants Yahoo! Video and peer-to-peer players like Kazaa. Just a month earlier, in October 2005, of the 470 sites in the category, YouTube had ranked in the thirty-ninth position, with only 0.17 per cent of visits to the category. YouTube's rise from the vast collection of unknown video sites didn't take years, or even months for that matter. The move from obscurity to ubiquity occurred in the span of just thirty-five days.

The first video posted on YouTube was entitled 'Me at the Zoo', an eighteen-second clip shot at the zoo in front of the elephant encosure posted by one of the YouTube founders, Jawed Karim. A few weeks later, when the site officially went into beta, in May 2005, it was averaging about 30,000 video views per day. By the overtake of Yahoo! Video in January 2006, YouTube was recording more than 25 million videos watched per day.[35]

If we apply the above chart to Rogers's diffusion curve, in the time period between the first video upload and the site launch in mid-December 2005, the visitors and uploaders to the site were most likely members of the Innovator segment, who, in trying out the service, established the novelty of creating their own content in the form of video files and uploading those files for the world to watch. Some time between November 2005 and January 2006 the diffusion of YouTube use moved from Innovator to Early Adopter, and then crossed over to the Early Majority.

I use the weekly and daily charts of YouTube's early success frequently when I describe why companies that compete in the online space need to make use of competitive intelligence data. In a world where market leadership can be upended in a matter of days, how can any company in their right mind operate blind to the competition around them?

It wasn't until a year later that we saw the connection between the YouTube growth chart and Rogers's diffusion curve. Hitwise data, when charted historically, could provide a visualization of how a new service, such as video uploads, moved across the segments that Rogers identified in the 1950s. Using another tool we've discussed before, clickstream analysis (a report that provides the top sites visited before and after a domain – or what website Internet users were on just prior to visiting YouTube and where they went immediately afterwards), we could also understand the mechanism of how word of this new site spread.

In October 2005, YouTube, still in beta form, received 52 per cent of its traffic from social networking sites like MySpace, Friendster, Xanga and even the new kid on the block, Facebook. Word of this new video site where users could create their own video content (or upload copyrighted content) was spreading through the online communities of high-school and college students – Innovators in the world of online video.

Within just one month, the method by which users arrived at the YouTube site began to shift dramatically. Traffic from email services (Web-based email accounts like Hotmail and Yahoo! Mail) were contributing more than 17 per cent of all traffic to the site, while social networking traffic declined to just 30 per cent. On the YouTube site, once users viewed a video, they had the ability to send an email to friends that included a link back to the video that they had just viewed. As Early Adopters took the baton from the Innovators, email was the tool they used to quickly spread the word about the new site and attract the Early Majority.

There were more clues about YouTube's meteoric rise hidden in the data. Along with social networking and email traffic, visits from Google were showing up in YouTube's clickstream in January 2006. Members of the Early Majority, hearing the buzz about YouTube, were finding the site by searching for it and for popular clips that they were hearing about. By looking at the top search terms that sent visitors to the site in January 2006, we could get an idea of what was igniting the interest of the Early Majority. For all the hype that was circulating in the media regarding the power of consumer-generated media, or videos created and uploaded by individuals, that's not what fuelled the rise of YouTube.

For the four weeks ending 28 January 2006, of the top ten searches sending traffic to YouTube, five of the terms were navigational searches (searches on the company name YouTube or the domain YouTube. com). The other five terms (number four: 'Lazy

Sunday'; number seven: 'Narnia Rap'; number eight: 'SNL Lazy Sunday'; number nine: 'Chronicles of Narnia SNL'; and number ten: 'SNL Lazy Sunday') all referred to the same video clip,[36] a skit from NBC's *Saturday Night Live,* featuring Chris Parnell and Andy Samberg, that aired the same week as YouTube's début. The skit, entitled 'Lazy Sunday', was a music video chronicling Parnell and Samberg's Sunday mission to catch the movie *The Chronicles of Narnia.*

NOW THAT WE UNDERSTOOD what drove the growth of YouTube, and could visualize the adoption of the new online technology by Innovators (visiting from social networks), Early Adopters (sharing the first clips via email) and Early Majority users (searching for a specific clip), there was an even more exciting prospect. Since Hitwise data on demographics and psychographics of visitors to websites is kept historically in snapshots of rolling four-week sections of time, it would be possible to take the diffusion-of-innovation analysis to the next level. By rolling back our data to those few weeks in December and January, we could identify the types of Internet users who made up the Early Adopters of online video sharing.

The basic demographics of age, gender, income and

region (by state) didn't surprise us. The largest group of users by age at this time was that of 18–24-year-olds (39 per cent). They earned under $60,000 per year (57 per cent). And more than 25 per cent of all visitors were based in California. Psychographic data from the Claritas PRIZM segmentation of visitors to the site gave us a much more detailed portrait of the on-line video Early Adopter.

One of the largest segments, representing more than 5 per cent of visitors to the site in this time frame, was the psychographic group Bohemian Mix. Members of this group, which Claritas describes as a collection of mobile urbanites living the most liberal lifestyle, are likely to live in funky terraced houses and are in general characterized as Early Adopters of entertainment and technology.

Excited by the discovery of a description of the potential Early Adopter, we performed the same analysis on a number of other Web 2.0 properties – like social photography site Flickr, social bookmark-ing sites like Digg and del.icio.us – and found that the Bohemian Mix was present in force on all these sites (and conspicuously missing from Web 1.0 coun-terpart sites). We also found that two other segments tended to appear alongside the Bohemian Mix in vis-iting cutting-edge online properties: the Money and Brains segment and the Young Digerati.

Through all of the information that Claritas had compiled about these three segments, along with what else we could glean on them from online behaviour, we got a very deep understanding of who the Early Adopter targets were.

THE BOHEMIAN MIX

The first segment, which is comprised of 2 million households in the United States, is the Bohemian Mix. This group is likely to live in urban areas, most likely in and around cities such as New York City and San Francisco. From the various surveys and other sources that Claritas adds to their segment data, we know that members of this segment are likely to read *New York* magazine and the *Wall Street Journal*, *Esquire* and the *New York Times*. They shop at stores such as Bloomingdale's, Saks Fifth Avenue and Banana Republic, and, perhaps providing the inspiration for their segment name, they index the highest for jobs in the arts, being more than three times as likely to work in that sector as the US population in general.

They also tend to be trendsetters in fashion (likely to watch the Style Network on digital cable) and in lifestyle (indexing high for driving Mini Coopers). This trendsetting also applies to new technology, as the Bohemian Mix is likely to try it out. All of these characteristics, taken together, describe a group that fits the bill for those who might be early in trying out a service like YouTube. While all of this data was compiled from survey results, we can also query our database of 1 million websites to see what Bohemian Mix Internet users might be likely to do online.

From their surfing behaviour, we know that they like to read news online, preferring to visit NYTimes. com and SFGate.com (the *San Francisco Chronicle* site) as their online newspaper. What doesn't show in the survey data is that this group also has a bent towards online gambling, visiting gaming sites like Bodog.com and offshore betting sites like BetUS. com. In terms of online interaction, the Bohemian Mix has moved on from the now mainstream social networks like MySpace and Facebook, preferring Google's fledgling network Orkut and the music-oriented social network site imeem.

MONEY AND BRAINS

Unlike their artistic Bohemian Mix counterparts, members of the Money and Brains segment, the second Early Adopter segment, tend to be affluent, holding advanced degrees and likely to work in legal, medical or management jobs. Like the Bohemian Mix, this is an urban segment, likely to live in Richmond

County, New York, but with its greatest presence in California, including San Francisco, San Mateo and Santa Clara counties.

Members of the Money and Brains segment also tend to be more conspicuous and status-conscious consumers, driving Mercedes Benzes and BMWs, and shopping at Nordstrom and Neiman Marcus. For media consumption, this group also reads the *New York Times,* but instead of watching the Style Network they are more likely to watch ESPN. Rather than read fashion magazines, members of this group would be more likely to pick up a *PC World* or *PC Magazine* at the newsstand.

Online, the Money and Brains segment stays true to their name, as heavy visitors to stock brokerage sites like Charles Schwab and Smith Barney, as well as financial information sites such as TheStreet.com and MarketWatch.com. Money and Brains people show a strong interest in sports, in contrast to the Bohemian Mix, with visits to ESPN.com, CBSSports-Line and Yahoo! Fantasy Sports. This segment's online behaviour also demonstrates its proclivity for travel, visiting airline websites like United.com, as well as travel review sites such as TripAdvisor.com. Perhaps online gambling is a thread that runs through online Early Adopter segments. One of the sites with the greatest concentration for the Money and Brains segment is called Covers.com and provides sports wagering information.

THE YOUNG DIGERATI

Of the three segments, the Young Digerati are the most affluent as well as the most tech-savvy. Members of this group tend to be on the urban fringe. They are highly educated and, among the groups, the most ethnically mixed. According to Claritas research, there are 1.3 million households in this group. Young Digerati people are likely to be employed as computer scientists. Their retail habits tend to be not as high end as the Money and Brains segment; this group is more likely to prefer brands such as Banana Republic and J.Crew. That same lack of high-end brand consciousness, however, doesn't transfer to vehicle preferences. This group is likely to own or lease a Mercedes, BMW or Range Rover.

The outstanding characteristic for the Young Digerati, however, is their interest in leveraging what they can from the Internet. Their online surfing behaviour confirms that. Of the top sites visited by this segment, Go Daddy's[37] Web-based email accounts is number one, indicating that members of this segment have registered their own domain names. They are also heavy Google users, the only group that registers high for use of Google Calendar, and, like the Bohemian Mix, they have a high representation in visits to Google's social network, Orkut. And like the other two groups, they also visit sports betting sites such as Bodog.com.

TOGETHER, THESE THREE GROUPS represent the Early Adopters for social networking sites like You-Tube, Flickr, Digg and del.icio.us. Once we discovered these groups and gained an understanding of who they are based on survey data and online behavioural patterns, we could help our clients build online marketing programmes that would attract Internet users most likely to act as a catalyst for word of mouth on any new online service. But there was an even more exciting potential use for this data.

If we roll our data backwards to identify the Early Adopters as we did with YouTube, we also have the capability of combining the Early Adopter segments together and asking what these segments are doing currently. For the first time, we have the data available to tell us what hot sites Early Adopters are visiting and possibly evangelizing today.

For example, above we identified that two of the segments, the Bohemian Mix and the Young Digerati, are overrepresented at, or more likely than the average Internet user to use, the Google social network, Orkut. Even though Orkut has great lineage in its parent company Google, the site, as of January

2008, ranks in the fifty-first position of all online social networks visited by US Internet users. Its market share of visits is a scant 0.17 per cent of the Social Networking category. While there are other factors at play in taking a site through the diffusion curve to mass adoption, the presence of Early Adopters on the Orkut site tells us that it might have a better chance than others to break out.

We can also use this form of screening analysis to identify higher-level trends. For example, if we narrow our reverse search to sites in the Entertainment-Multimedia category and just look at those sites with a high percentage of our three segments, trends emerge. In January 2008, we can see that the collective group of Early Adopter segments are interested in capturing the streaming videos[38] that are part of YouTube and saving them as files that can be played regardless of an available Internet connection.

We also know that our group of Early Adopters is willing to test other online video sites beyond You-Tube, trying out services like Veoh and Wikimedia Commons. This willingness to try new services demonstrates that this particular group of Internet users, while continuing to use mainstream services online, is always on the lookout for something better. Along with searching for improvements to current online services, our Early Adopter segments are also willing to try out new social network paradigms. This group is particularly interested in trying webcam-based social network services such as Stickam.com and Webcamnow.com. Finally, we also know that this group is on the forefront of the integration of interactive entertainment and the Internet, visiting sites like Yahoo!'s Bix service, which combine social networking and consumer-generated videos with online talent contests. Users of Bix record videos of themselves and upload those videos to compete in the contests. Karaoke is a particularly popular category of contest for the service.

IF WE CAN VISUALIZE the second segment in Rogers's diffusion curve, then it should be possible to isolate the other segments of the graph as well. The Early Majority are the next segment in the adoption chain. According to Rogers, they are open to new ideas and interact frequently with their peers, but unlike the Early Adopter, the Early Majority person is seldom thought of as an opinion or thought leader.

While they may not hold the marketing powers of the Early Adopter, the Early Majority, if present in the segmentation of a site immediately after the Early Adopter segment, would be a good indication that an online trend is gaining traction.

By performing the same analysis that we did to identify the Early Adopter segments, we went back to our Web 2.0 sites and examined what segments spiked immediately after the Early Adopters. One segment showed the most promise: the still urban but less affluent segment number twenty-nine, which Claritas refers to as the 'American Dreams'. While the Early Adopter segments represented upper- and upper-middle-class urban households, the American Dreams household is solidly in the middle class. This group also tends to show far greater ethnic diversity than the other Early Adopter segments.

The American Dreams' media and shopping behaviour puts them right on the cusp of the Early Majority in technology adoption. They index high for shopping at computer stores, and are technologically forward for their interest in streaming music stations on Internet radio. Their online behaviours reflect what the Claritas data shows. They, like the Young Digerati, tend to shop for computers and electronics online. Members of their household also visit alternative social networks such as hi5 and former leader in the space Friendster.

As we build on our understanding of how Internet data can help us visualize the diffusion of new technology, robust models that identify the ebb and flow of behavioural segments' usage will revolutionize our ability to market and track the potential of new services that are brought into the marketplace.

THERE IS A SECOND curve in the study of diffusion of innovations that sheds light on the speed at which new technologies are adopted.

When you chart the cumulative adoption of a new technology, the resulting curve resembles an S shape, with the initial adoption relatively slow compared to the steep growth in cumulative use as the product or service moves into the mainstream. The inflection point that occurs can also be described as the tipping point that Malcolm Gladwell introduced us to in his landmark book by the same name.

The adoption of new social networks and video-sharing sites is just the tip of the iceberg of what trends may be predicted using Internet behavioural data. The same concepts that we've applied here can also be applied in the fashion industry (measuring the segments who visit fashion-forward sites or the sites of manufacturers whose new items become the latest fashion trend), to media consumption behaviours, even to predicting the tipping point of a new musical band or artist. Which is exactly where the next chapter takes us, across the pond to a small music club in Sheffield, England.

CHAPTER 11

Super-Connectors and Predicting the Next Rock Star

A post-punk indie rock band called the Arctic Monkeys played their first gig on 13 June 2003 at the Grapes, a nondescript pub on Trippett Lane in Sheffield. If geography was any predictor of the potential for this post-punk revival group of school friends, they were in good company. The town of Sheffield has a rich history as the starting place for musicians such as Pulp, Def Leppard, Human League, Joe Cocker and Thompson Twins.

On this summer night a crowd gathered in the minuscule upstairs, a venue that, with its small stage and band equipment, could barely fit a capacity crowd of sixty. After a few performances, the Arctic Monkeys were still undiscovered, so a friend of the band burned demo CDs of their music and began handing them out during this performance, thereby launching a gratis grassroots publicity campaign in the grand indie rock DIY tradition. After a few more shows, the band was playing Sheffield Forum, to a large crowd of fans who knew lyrics that Alex Turner (their lead singer and guitarist) hadn't even memorized. The band couldn't understand it, but there was a reason their fan base had been swelling: Tracks from the demos they'd been handing out at gigs had been spreading like wildfire.[39]

'What's happened has been proper hysterical,' recounts Turner. 'If I say "phenomenon" it sounds like I'm right up my own arse, but we'd be daft to act like we didn't realize how incredible the last year's been. When it all started we were like "What's going off here?" . . . I used to work in a bar at venues and it really annoyed me when bands would say "We've got CDs for sale at the back, three pounds each." You'd think "F— off, who do you think you are?" We had this one time where people were literally running up to the stage clambering for these demos, a right frenzy, and we were thinking "F'ing hell, this is cool." [40] In a 2005 interview while on tour in the United States, the band admitted that they didn't even know how to upload their music to the Internet. 'The fans just used to send them [song files] to each other, which didn't bother us because we never made those demos to make money or anything. We were giving them away free anyway – that was a better way for people to hear them. And it made the gigs better, because people knew the words and came and sang along."[41]

To hear the band's account of their rapid rise to local fame, you would quickly conclude that their success was a very fortuitous accident. The music was good, but the free demo CDs were in short supply. So how did their fan base mushroom so quickly? The fans, so the story goes, eager to share news of their new favourite band, unwittingly created a new music distribution phenomenon. They began uploading tracks from the demo CDs to Internet file-sharing sites for the world to hear. So was there a mythical first fan, a tech-savvy lone enthusiast who first uploaded the band's tracks online? That remains a mystery, but at least one such event can be traced back to two guys who tagged along to film the band very early in their career and who, according to Turner, put the band's songs online for fans and potential fans to listen to for free. The word simply spread from there.

The Arctic Monkeys were unknowingly at the epicentre of Web 2.0, which was premised on the idea that consumers generate the media. Content in the form of editorials, music and even video was shifting from large media publishers to the newly empowered consumer. Over the next year, one website would change the face of the Internet and lead to the Zeitgeist phenomenon that became known as the MySpace Generation.

MYSPACE: CHANGING THE PLAYING FIELD

In Southern California during that same summer of 2003, friends Tom Anderson and Chris DeWolf assembled a small group of programmers they had earlier met at a file-sharing service they worked for called Xdrive. The goal: to create a new generation of file-sharing websites. The team cobbled together the best components of file-sharing sites (Craigslist, Evite and MP3.com), and the result was a site that allowed users to create their own page on the service, upload photos and music files, and, most importantly, invite friends to connect and visit their site, creating an online social network.

The site was called MySpace.

According to DeWolf, music was a big catalyst in the early success of MySpace. 'We launched MySpace in 2003, inviting local bands and club owners to post pages and allowing other users to become their "friends" . . . The bands turned out to be our best marketing tool. All these creative people became ambassadors for MySpace by using us as their de facto promotional platform. People like to talk about music, so the bands set up a natural environment to communicate.'[42] To ensure the success of MySpace, the founders reached out to key influencers on other social networking sites, like Friendster. One of those influencers was a *Playboy* 'Cyber-girl' who went by the moniker Tila Tequila. She proved critical to MySpace's success, and MySpace proved just as critical to hers.

MEET THE SUPER-CONNECTOR

But before we get to Tila Tequila, let's back up and consider what we talk about when we talk about social networks. A good place to start is with the work of Robin Dunbar, a British anthropologist who specializes in the socialization patterns of primates. His most famous contribution to the study of social networks is something called the 'Rule of 150'.[43] The idea, according to Dunbar, is that there is a naturally occurring limit to the number of meaningful contacts each of us has, and that number is 150.[44] To prove his point, Dunbar surveyed individuals about how many Christmas cards they sent out in the previous holiday season. Operating on the assumption that our Christmas card lists represent an approximation of the individuals within our social network, Dunbar found that the mean response was 153.5 meaningful contacts.[45]

However, there is a select group of us whose social networks have far exceeded Dunbar's rule of 150.

Malcolm Gladwell profiled one such woman for *The New Yorker*, in a piece that was later included in his landmark book *The Tipping Point*.

In the profile, Gladwell introduced us to a Chicago grandmother named Lois Weisberg, Chicago's commissioner of community affairs. Weisberg was a perfect example of how individuals with wide social circles are responsible for the 'small world phenomenon'. This phenomenon is commonly known as six degrees of separation, or the idea that anyone in the world will be connected to any other through a maximum of six people. And what was special about Weisberg, we learned, was that she had an unquenchable thirst for establishing connections between people.

Gladwell wrote:

> The epicentre of the [Chicago] city administration . . . Lois is far from being the most important or the most powerful person in Chicago. But if you connect all the dots that constitute the vast apparatus of government and influence and interest groups in the city of Chicago, you'll end up coming back to Lois again and again. Lois is a connector.[46]

What's important, moreover, was what motivated Weisberg to discover and connect with so many people. 'She doesn't network for the sake of networking,' said one acquaintance. 'I think she just has the confidence that all the people in the world, whether she has met them or not, are in her Rolodex already, and that all she has to do is figure out how to reach them and she'll be able to connect with them.'[47] In just one telling example of her obsession with bringing people together, Weisberg coordinated efforts to scatter 300 table-tennis tables around town, luring all sorts of people who normally wouldn't cross paths, 'businessmen, tourists and kids to square off in a friendly competition that left a reservoir of good feeling long after the games ended'.[48]

THE LANDSCAPE HAS SHIFTED since Gladwell wrote *The Tipping Point*. The advent of online social networks that live and die on MySpace, YouTube and Facebook (and their countless imitators) has, as we shall discover, created a new breed of connectors. And setting aside for a moment the nature of the friendships and connections birthed via these networks, it is important to note that this new category of connectors count their 'friends' in the thousands and even higher.

When Jonathan Abrams founded the first online social network, Friendster, in 2002, the site created a viral mission among its users. The mission: to accumulate as many friends as possible. The concept became known as the 'circle of friends'. By late 2003 expansion in user-base and usage had created unforeseen demands on the infrastructure of the site, a victim of its own success. Growing frustrated with poor performance, users began abandoning the service. Amid Friendster's decline in popularity, several other social networks began to spring up in its wake: Facebook, Bebo and, most notably, MySpace.

All of a sudden, Dunbar's rule of 150 seemed quaint. In the land of MySpace it was not uncommon to find individuals who numbered their friends in the tens and even hundreds of thousands. In a certain sense, the advent of online social networks had both created and enabled a new breed of connectors. We'll call this new breed 'super-connectors'.

Measured solely by number of connections, Lois Weisberg could easily have prove the exception to Dunbar's Rule of 150. That said, she is no match for the archetype super-connector, a foul-mouthed e-vixen who goes by the online moniker of Tila Tequila. Born Tila Nguyen, Ms Tequila, as of the writing of this book, is the most popular personality on MySpace, counting 1,645,873 friends within her network and over a quarter of a billion visits to her personal profile.

Tequila was lured to MySpace by its founder, Tom Anderson, who presciently recognized her role on

Friendster as an influencer. It didn't take much convincing; Tequila had been booted from Friendster several times for her 'in-your-face' behaviour. 'I joined MySpace in September 2003,' Tequila recalls. 'At that time no one was on there at all. I felt like a loser while all the cool kids were at some other school. So I mass e-mailed between 30,000 and 50,000 people and told them to come over. Everybody joined overnight.'[49]

Through her online connections, Tequila has leveraged her online celebrity into an empire, including a cable television hosting gig on Fuse TV's *Pants-Off Dance-Off*, a mobile phone company sponsorship, a line of clothing and a soon-to-be released album on the A&M Records label. Verses to her MySpace single 'F* You Man', a single distributed solely through the site, give a glimpse inside the self-directed world of Tila Tequila as she attempts to persuade other women on MySpace that she's not after their men.

While no one would argue that Tequila's network of friends are neither 'friends' in the sense of Dunbar's rule of 150 nor the quality connections that Lois Weisberg created, it is clear that her rise to stardom was fuelled by these cyber connections and that the connections have real currency that goes far beyond ego boosting. The rise of online social networking has, for the purpose of social epidemics and tipping points, laid waste to the notion of 150 connections and given rise to a whole new definition of social power, leverage and, in turn, trends.

Now let's revisit the qualitative differences between Tequila and Weisberg. Traditional, pre-Web 2.0 connectors connected to connect. For Weisberg and her ilk, connecting Friend A with a love of antique handbags with Friend B who operates a vintage handbag stall at Chicago's flea market was where the magic happened. Bringing people together via shared affinities, mutual business interests or simply that romantic *je ne sais quoi* was what old-school connectors lived for.

Now Tequila: In an MSNBC interview with Tucker Carlson, when asked about her success, she responded, 'I've always had this thing, where, like, I want attention from everybody . . . It's pretty much being a hustler if you know what that is.' When asked what she does all day, her answer: 'I don't sleep at all; taking over the world is not an easy job.' And how much time does she spend on MySpace? 'About twenty-four hours a day.' In other words, Tequila's millions of connections are primarily a function of her vanity and self-interest, of her desire for fame and fortune.

But what is exciting for our purpose about the appearance of super-connectors is that they, like Tequila, live and transact online. As Gladwell points out in *The Tipping Point*, connectors are one of the necessary ingredients in the start of social epidemics and trends. Today, super-connectors play the same role but with a far greater power, which they leverage via their vast online networks. If we track the aggregate behaviour of super-connectors and the rest of the online social networking world, we can quantify early stages of an epidemic or trend – we can see the tipping point. In short, we – businesses, armchair anthropologists and trackers of Zeitgeist – can predict what will happen in the offline world by looking at what is going on, under our very noses, online.

FINDING THE TIPPING POINT ONLINE

As we saw in Chapter 9, I had predicted the winner of the UK hit show *Strictly Come Dancing*, a reality-based ballroom dancing competition. The story had unfolded this way: Using the volume of searches on the various contestants as an indication of a contestant's popularity, in front of a crowd of 200 Hitwise clients at a search seminar I'd predicted that cricketer Mark Ramprakash would win the season. Heather Hopkins, our London research head, called to let me know that I hadn't made a laughing stock out of myself or the company; based solely on search behaviour, we'd made yet another accurate reality show prediction.

But Heather was on to an even more exciting prediction method. An avid fan of Malcolm Gladwell's work, Heather reasoned that if connectors' activities are related to the adoption of a new trend, and we could see the aggregate activity from the new super-connectors through our data, shouldn't we be able to predict trends before anyone else?

In October 2003, the same time that MySpace launched, the Arctic Monkeys released their first single, 'I Bet You Look Good on the Dance Floor', on Domino Records, a small independent label run out of the founders' flat in London. The song soared to the number one position on the UK singles chart, all without the aid of a major record label.

Soon after the Arctic Monkeys' first single débuted, Heather began to look at how a relatively obscure band could rise to stardom without the backing of a major label. She started by examining the visits to the band's official website around the time of their first single release.

When they're online, Internet users create a trail of the sites they visit. For any of the 800,000 sites on which we collect information, we can see the sites visited just before and just after the site in question – the clickstream. There are a number of investigative tools at our disposal, but in this case the clickstreams for MySpace and a band's official website held the key to discovering the collective conscience of the super-connectors and their minions.

While lines formed outside of the Grapes in Sheffield, buzz began to build online, fuelled by uploaded MP3 files, no doubt originating with the first demo CDs handed out in Sheffield. MySpace users began posting Arctic Monkey songs to their profile pages. When super-connectors like the Tila Tequilas of the social networking world began including Arctic Monkeys clips on their profile pages, interest in the Arctic Monkeys spread instantaneously.

In order to understand the Arctic Monkeys' success, we needed a place to start our analysis. While search-term popularity worked well for reality television predictions, it was only one piece of the puzzle this time. What we wanted to find was the impact of the super-connectors on the Arctic Monkeys' success, and to do that we needed an anchor for the band's online persona. Thankfully, no self-respecting band in today's music world can exist without an official band website. The Arctic Monkeys' website, www.arcticmonkeys.com, was our anchor.

The secret to tracking the effect of a super-connector on a band's success lay hidden in the data that told the story of how users navigated to the band's official website. Like the air current created by a butterfly's wings affecting weather patterns across the globe, a Sheffield clubber uploading a music clip to her My-Space profile, from a demo CD she'd received that evening at the Grapes, could similarly be the one responsible for starting the chain reaction that launched the Arctic Monkeys into stardom.

The mechanics of music promotion in a post-Arctic Monkeys world is very simple. Today, in addition to the official band website, most musicians create a profile on MySpace. Along with their bio, bands' websites include a tour schedule, photos and music files that are playable within the MySpace domain. The next step is critical. A smart band will then invite key MySpace influencers – hand-picked loudmouths who do the work of the original Arctic Monkeys fans – or super-connectors, to their page to listen and download their music. Using a shotgun approach, an invitation to thousands will yield success among a few key, influential users. As those users upload the band's files to their pages for others to hear, a viral social network is created around the bands' music. It's like the twenty-first-century version of getting an A-list director attached to a young, untested writer's screenplay.

At some point, as their music files continue to multiply online and visits to the band's MySpace profile ramp up, word spreads beyond the walls of social networks to music fans across the world. Internet users visiting blogs and mainstream music fan sites catch the buzz about the new UK band and turn to search engines to find out more about the artists and their music. As with our reality TV contestants, searches for the Arctic Monkeys begin to ramp up, giving indication of their rising popularity.

Returning to the clickstream of visits to the band's website, as mainstream Internet users continue to find more information on their songs and appearances, the visits to the website from search engines surpass those visits from the buzz of social networking.

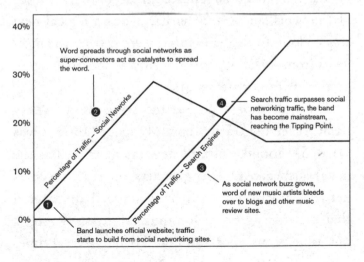

**Finding the Tipping Point
for Music Artists Online**

Word spreads through social networks as super-connectors act as catalysts to spread the word.

Percentage of Traffic - Social Networks

Percentage of Traffic - Search Engines

Search traffic surpasses social networking traffic, the band has become mainstream, reaching the Tipping Point.

As social network buzz grows, word of new music artists bleeds over to blogs and other music review sites.

Band launches official website; traffic starts to build from social networking sites.

There in the intersection of the two sources of traffic lies the tipping point.

Record executives might rely on their hunches in signing a new artist to their label. Some might rely on market research or even algorithms that factor pitch, tone, chord progression and rhythm to pick the next hot artist. In today's age of the super-connector, hidden in the surfing habits of music fans lie the secrets of an artist's potential popularity. Observed behaviour in the form of Internet visits from MySpace and other social networks to a band's official page could be the crystal ball that the entertainment industry has been looking for.

After testing our theory on a number of new bands, and seeing the repeated trade-off between social network and search visits, it was a logical next step to look to the bands that were getting the most visits from social networking sites as the first step to predicting tomorrow's stars.

The first time I pulled the list of top twenty bands receiving traffic from MySpace Music, I was startled. I found a mix of new talent as well as the usual suspects. Drawing charts on search versus network traffic for each band's site, I discovered that the tipping point for musical artists wasn't a one-time occurrence, but could occur several times throughout their career, as they released new albums and went on tour.

Of course, sometimes our data revelations are a result of serendipity. Thinking about Heather's discovery, I was searching for some other examples of a similar tipping point. Driving down Market Street in San Francisco, a local club marquee caught my eye; it was advertising the upcoming show dates for a band called Fall Out Boy.

I knew I had seen that band name before; the official band site was one of the top sites in our Band category, and if memory served me, it was the band receiving the most traffic from the MySpace Music site.

Fall Out Boy is a Chicago pop-punk band started in 2001 in the suburban town of Wilmette, Illinois. Fall Out Boy's style is most often described as 'emo', a brand of punk-influenced rock that is widely believed to have its roots in the Washington, DC, hardcore scene of the 1980s and '90s. The name 'emo' is derived from 'emotional' and reflects the band's propensity to produce emotional outbursts during performances.

While they are hardly a household name, the band's second album, *From Under the Cork Tree*, reached the number nine position on the *Billboard* album chart in 2005. But in the gap between that album's release and their next album, which was due in February 2007, the band began to slip into obscurity, dropping from a top five position in band sites visited in the United States down to the number 410 position in October 2006.

As the band hit bottom, their lowest ranking in the Hitwise Music: Bands and Artists category in two years, searches and traffic from search engines for Fall Out Boy also reached a two-year low. But something else caught my eye – visits to the band's site from social networks were reaching an all-time high. The super-connector buzz surrounding the band and their upcoming new album was nearing fever pitch.

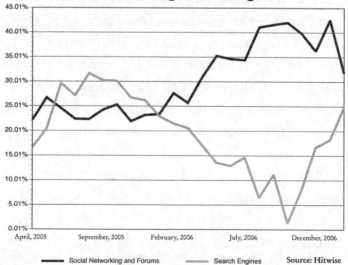

Market Share of Visits to the Social Networks and Search Engines Categories

Social Networking and Forums — Search Engines — Source: Hitwise

By the last week in October 2006, traffic from social networks had reached its pinnacle – and search-engine traffic, so recently on the downswing, was increasing at a fast clip. The writing was on the wall: Fall Out Boy was heading for its second tipping point. Based on the amplitude of traffic from sites like MySpace (42 per cent of all Fall Out Boy traffic in October), I predicted that the band's February 2007 album release would be a chart-topper.

Several months later, the band's third album, *Infinity on High*, reached the number one position on the *Billboard* Top 200 in the first week after its release, selling 260,000 copies, going platinum the same month it was released.

Who We Are and Why It Matters

At times the number of stories hidden within the data, stories that I still haven't discovered, overwhelms me. Over these pages we've covered a very disparate collection of data stories, from the underside of the Internet in visits to adult entertainment and gambling sites to the popularity of prom dresses, women wrestlers and the Arctic Monkeys. Taken all together, what does all of this mean?

The idea to look for a correlation between topics or the idea to gather insight on a particular topic can come from several different sources. For me this usually happens in the background – something I hear on the radio or television, or the fragment of an overheard conversation.

One morning while I was getting ready for work, I had the television on in the background and heard something that piqued my interest. A commercial was playing for Mirapex, a drug for a newly discovered medical condition: restless leg syndrome, or RLS for short. RLS is defined by the National Institute of Neurological Disorders as a disorder 'characterized by an uncomfortable sensation in the legs and an uncontrollable urge to move in an effort to relieve these feelings'. As a chronic foot-tapper, I was incredulous that such a condition existed, while at the same time I couldn't resist questioning whether I had contracted the disease.

As I turned away from the television, the voice-over reading through the video equivalent of boilerplate said something quite remarkable: 'If you suffer from a gambling addiction, this drug may not be for you.'

Huh? I had to hit the rewind on our TiVo to make sure of what I had just heard. Within a few minutes I was logged into the Hitwise tool, attempting to find some form of positive correlation between RLS and online gambling. Disappointed that I couldn't find any increase in gambling visits online to correspond with a massive spike on searches of 'restless leg syndrome', I returned to medical research literature. As I tried to find the connection, I discovered that a study at Johns Hopkins had established the link between the drug and compulsive behaviours.[50]

As I continued my research online, I found an interesting opportunity for more analysis. Research unearthed several sceptics of this new disease, with one study asking the specific critical question: Is media coverage of this new disease actually making us (or at least making us think we're) sick?[51]

Charting the volume of searches on the term 'restless leg syndrome' indicated a dramatic spike in searches on the term when the FDA had approved the RLS drug 'Requip'. With my foot tapping in anticipation, I charted searches on symptoms of RLS such as 'shaking leg', to see if the searches predated the run of commercials for drugs treating the disease: nothing.

While I didn't find dispositive data on the connection between drug release and disease awareness, the quick morning exercise of turning to Internet data to find a potential connection reminded me of the value that lay hidden in our Internet browsing and search behaviour. In this case the media coverage of a new drug for a new disease didn't cause an increase in searches on the drug, but on the condition itself, proving that information disseminated via news stories and commercials can cause us to respond online in a certain way. The data provides us with a view into the feedback loop.

In our increasingly connected lives, we're bombarded with news and information from a multitude of channels (television, print, radio and the Internet), some useful, some not so useful. It gets interesting, as in the case with RLS, when we react to that information by interacting with the source itself. What information we react to and how, when viewed collectively, reveals insight into what affects us.

From a business perspective, having a view into the feedback loop is invaluable – from the simple, tactical use of planning when to promote products online, such as prom dresses and engagement rings, to the visualization of Malcolm Gladwell's tipping point in the charting of search versus social-network traffic to a band's official website.

Aside from learning more about ourselves from the pseudo-conversations that we have with search engines like Google about our fears, or trying to understand something that's unclear to us, our Internet usage data allows us to see, on a massive scale, theories such as the Diffusion of Innovation that Bryce Ryan experienced in the Iowa cornfields. Now we can see those same diffusions play out with sites such as YouTube, MySpace and Facebook, and even identify the members of each group that cause technology to spread through our society.

But when you get back to the question of why this

data matters, what is very clear in the observations I've made in my four years studying Internet behaviour patterns is that the Internet itself is changing the way we experience the world.

To see the change that I'm talking about, look no further than the newspaper industry. If you roll the clock back to the mid-nineties, most of us consumed our news at the breakfast table. When we opened up the morning newspaper, the contents were, for lack of a better term, news to us. In the evenings we'd supplement that with a dose of local and national television news coverage. In rare instances, such as national tragedies, assassination attempts or other breaking news stories, if we were close to a television, we received news as it was breaking.

Today, with news websites, RSS news feeds and blogs, we have the ability to receive all of our news on-demand in a format and a place that suits our needs – on our desktops, laptops and, for some, on Internet-enabled phones such as the iPhone. For the majority of us who are 'wired', when we open up the morning paper today, most of the content is old news, items that we've read the previous afternoon and evening.

The disruption wrought by the Internet on the news industry doesn't end there. Classifieds, once a key revenue stream for newspapers, are no contest for the likes of online classifieds like Craigslist or for the massive marketplace of buyers and sellers that transact on eBay. Even obituaries have become obsolete as sites like Legacy.com provide an interactive searchable database of the deceased. Finally, the content itself is no longer reserved for the newsroom; the rise of citizen journalism has proven that news reporting is no longer under its domain.

Changes in the newspaper industry are just the beginning. As we continue to become more interactive with the information on our screens and at our fingertips, the way we live our lives will change, whether making purchases, decisions or even friends.

Understanding how we change will be paramount to businesses' success, as they adapt to the market and serve its evolving needs. What are Internet users doing online each day, and how will that change tomorrow, next month or next year? If you don't know, your only recourse will be to guess or to apply traditional business rules that were developed prior to the new information age.

Why is the analysis of our collective Internet behaviour so important? If for no other reason, it's about understanding ourselves and how we are constantly adapting in our rapidly evolving world. Simply stated, if you want to understand the new connected world and how we choose to live in it, look no further than our Internet behaviour; after all, we are what we click.

NOTES

CHAPTER 1. PPC – PORN, PILLS AND CASINOS

1. Ron Jackson, *DM Journal*, 9 December 2006.
2. Ibid.
3. Ibid.
4. John Leland, 'Suffering the Pornographers', *New York Times*, 31 September 2004.
5. 'Man May Have Sent 2 Billion Viagra Spam Emails', *USA Today*, 13 September 2006, http://www.usatoday.com/tech/news/2006-09-13-viagra-spam_x.html.

CHAPTER 2. GETTING TO WHAT WE REALLY THINK

6. Peverill Squire, 'Why the 1936 *Literary Digest* Poll Failed', *Public Opinion Quarterly*, 52 (1988), pp. 125–33.

7. It should be noted that teen fashion readers are more likely to be online, which may skew the clickstream for other online fashion properties.

CHAPTER 3. PROM IN JANUARY

8. 'Teens Spending Billions for Prom Magic', Associated Press, 27 May 2003.

9. Patricia Leavy, *Iconic Events* (Lanham, MD: Lexington Books, 2007), p. 178.

CHAPTER 4. FAILED RESOLUTIONS AND THE FALSE HOPE SYNDROME

10. John C. Norcross, Marci S. Mrykalo and Matthew D. Blagys, 'Auld Lang Syne: Success predictors, change processes, and self-reported outcomes of New Year's resolvers and nonresolvers', *Journal of Clinical Psychology* 58, no. 4 (2002).

11. IBM Consumer Media Survey, http://www-03 .ibm.com/industries/media/doc/content/landing/2507292111.html.

12. Sanford C. Bernstein Research, 'Pipe Dreams', May 2004.

CHAPTER 5. CELEBRITY WORSHIP SYNDROME

13. Margaret Gibson, 'Some Thoughts on Celebrity

Deaths, Steve Irwin and the Issue of Public Mourning', *Mortality* 12, no. 1 (2007): 1–3.

14. According to *Ask Men* magazine, Perez Hilton changed the name of his blog to PerezHilton. com due to legal pressure from the *New York Post*. http://www.askmen.com/men/business_ politics_60/87c_perez_hilton.html

CHAPTER 6. WHAT ARE YOU AFRAID OF? AND OTHER TELLING QUESTIONS

15. Kessler *et al.*, 'Social Phobia Subtypes in the National Comorbidity Survey', *American Journal of Psychiatry* 155 (May 1998): 613–19.

16. http://www.changethatsrightnow.com/problem _detail.asp? SDID=1404:1595

17. R.C. Kessler, W.T. Chiu, O. Demler and E.E. Walters, 'Prevalence, severity, and comorbidity of twelve-month DSM-IV disorders in the National Comorbidity Survey Replication (NCS-R)', *Archives of General Psychiatry* 62, no. 6 (June 2005): 617–27.

18. http://www.nimh.nih.gov/health/topics/social -phobia/index.shtml

19. The website PostSecret.blogspot.com has inter- mittently allowed submissions in the form of comments, and eventually through a separate section of the website, the PostSecret Community.

20. The fictional street in the hit ABC television show *Desperate Housewives*.

CHAPTER 7. WEB WHO.0

21. http://encarta.msn.com/encyclopedia_761551647_3/Encyclopedia.html

22. http://en.wikipedia.org/wiki/History_of_Wikipedia. Given the volatile nature of Wikipedia (i.e., anyone can edit the contents of the site at any time), this chapter will have the only incidences of Wikipedia as a reference in this book; and due to the nature of Wikipedia, I can't guarantee that what was referenced during the writing of this book will exist in the same form when you read this.

23. Ibid.

24. Number of Eiffel Tower photos on Flickr on 18 December 2007.

25. http://www.wired.com/wired/archive/12.10/tail_pr.html

26. http://www.useit.com/alertbox/participation_inequality.html

27. TripAdvisor's consumer rating service is built on a ranking of 1–5, with 1 being the lowest quality score and 5 being the highest.

28. 'The economics of *Groundhog Day*', posted 8/30/2006, http://www.mises.org/story/2289.

29. *New Yorker,* 5 July 1993, p.61.

CHAPTER 8. DATA ROCKS AND THE
TELEVISION–INTERNET CONNECTION

30. According to Direct Newsline; Ward's, 20 April
2005, the first Pontiac Solstice Special Edition
cars sold out within forty-one minutes of the
commercial airing. More than 20,000 visitors to
the site signed up for the waiting list to purchase
a Pontiac Solstice.

31. The SEO industry is divided into two types of
optimizers. The White Hats employ above-
board practices in line with search-engine
policies to get their clients the best placement in
search results. The other camp are the Black Hat
SEOs, which have various schemes within their
arsenal to raise a client's ranking in organic
results.

CHAPTER 9. WOMEN WRESTLERS AND
ARBITRAGING FINANCIAL MARKETS

32. I realize that there may be some demographic
difference between the show viewer who would
vote via telephone versus the one who would vote
online, but I reasoned that even phone-in viewers
might search on a contestant if they're true fans
and want more info on their favourite dancer.

Chapter 10. Finding the Early Adopters

33. Everett M. Rogers, *Diffusion of Innovations* (New York: Free Press, 1995), p. 283.

34. Ibid, p. 284.

35. Kevin Allison, *Financial Times*, 10 April 2006.

36. Between 17 December 2005, and 20 February 2006 the clip was viewed more than 5 million times on YouTube.

37. GoDaddy.com is a domain registration and web hosting company.

38. Sites like YouTube stream their video content. This method of video delivery requires that you be connected to the Internet, and replaying the file requires that you either retain or reinitiate an Internet connection. Several software programs have surfaced on the Internet that enable users to capture and save video files, usually in violation of copyright laws.

Chapter 11. Super-Connectors and Predicting the Next Rock Star

39. Arctic Monkeys biography, www.ilikemusic.com.

40. 'Arctic Monkeys in Concert', www.npr.org, 26 March 2006.

41. Dave Park, 'Arctic Monkeys aren't fooling around (Part 1)', *Prefix Magazine*, 21 November 2005, www.prefixmag.com.

42. Chris DeWolf, 'MySpace Cowboys', CNN Money.com, 4 November 2006.

43. R. I. M. Dunbar, 'Neocortex size as a constraint on group size in primates', *Journal of Human Evolution* 22: 469–93. The rule of 150 is the theoretical cognitive limit of individuals with whom any one person can maintain stable relationships.

44. R. A. Hill and R. I. M. Dunbar, 'Social Network Size in Humans', *Human Nature* 14, no. 1: 53–70.

45. Ibid, p. 57.

46. Malcolm Gladwell, 'Six Degrees of Lois Weisberg', *New Yorker,* 11 January 1999.

47. Ibid.

48. Christopher Conte, 'Culture and Whimsy', *Governing,* November 2001.

49. Lev Grossman, 'Power to the People', *TIME,* 17 December 2006.

EPILOGUE. WHO WE ARE AND WHY IT MATTERS

50. *Archives of Neurology,* July 2005.

51. *Public Library of Science Medicine,* April 2006.

GLOSSARY

All Categories: Includes the 172 industry categories
tracked by Hitwise. When used in charts, 'all
categories' refers to a site or category's market
share of visits compared to visits to all sites
within the Hitwise database.

All Sites: Includes all websites visited (over 1 million) by US Internet users across all 172 Hitwise
categories except Adult, ISPs and Ad Servers.

Clickstream: A report that details what sites or
categories of sites are visited just prior to a site
or category and what sites are visited immediately after a visit to that same site or category.

Demographics: Refers to a measure of gender, age,
household income and regional distribution by
state for visitors to a site or category.

Market Share: The percentage of all visits or page requests to a particular online market sector that is received by the individual website.

MOSAIC: A geodemographic segmentation system that divides the US population into twelve groups and fifty types based on unique behavioural characteristics.

PRIZM: A segmentation system from Claritas that is based on geodemographics, PRIZM segments are also represented in two groups, Lifestyle and Social Group, which are comprised of multiple PRIZM segments.

Psychographics: A system that groups individuals based on behaviour, beliefs and unique demographic characteristics.

Search-Term Breadth: Refers to the number of search terms that contain a specific term or phrase compared to the number of specific search terms in a given period of time.

User Visits: A series of page requests by a visitor without thirty consecutive minutes of inactivity, identified by a collection of page requests from a unique identifier.

Volume of Searches: Refers to the number of searches on a given term or phrase compared to all searches in a given time frame.

INDEX

A&E Television Networks
130–1
About.com 118
Abrams, Jonathan 265
AdultFanFiction.net 29
Advani, Deepak 50, 51
advertisements
diet 98–9, 100–2
embedded (product
placement) 107–8, 203–6
sponsored listings 207–8
television commercials 44,
102, 107, 206–10
affiliate partners 42–3
Affluent Suburbia segment
190–1
Alertbox 174
'all categories' 295
'all sites' 295
AltaVista 239
Altos research 218
Amazon.com 42–3, 218, 238
American Idol 121, 226
Anderson, Chris 173–4
Anderson, Tom 33, 262, 266–7
Apprentice, The 203–6
arbitrage *see* data arbitrage
Arctic Monkeys 259–62, 270–2

Ask.com 215, 216

Back Dorm Boys 167–8
Barba, Antonella 121
Battelle, John 200
Bebo 266
BetUS.com 251
Biggest Loser, The 106–7, 109,
118
bikinis 104
Bix 256
blogs 173
of author 106
celebrity 122, 133–8, 192–3
participation in 174
political 61–4, 192
Bodog.com 251, 254
Bohemian Mix segment 249,
250–1
Bossip.com 133, 137
brand marketing 50–3
brand searches 202–3

Cahill, Jannie 90
Carlson, Tucker 268
cars 203–10
CBSNews.com 64, 65
celebrities 119, 121–40

Anna Nicole Smith 121, 122, 127–30
attitudes of men vs. women toward 132–3
blogs and 122, 133–8, 192–3
deaths of 127–8
sex tapes by 126, 127
Celebrity Worship Scale 124–6, 134, 138
Centers for Disease Control (CDC) 54–5
Christianity 163
Claritas 59, 77–8, 129, 137, 249, 250, 253, 257, 296
classifieds 192, 283–4
clickstream data 61, 270–1, 295
on magazine sites 66–8
on political sites 64–6
on YouTube 246, 247
Clinton, Hillary 56
Clooney, George 133, 134
CNBC 59, 227, 232–5
CNN 47
cognitive dissonance 24–5, 49–50, 99–100, 146
Cohen, Stephen Michael 20
confessional websites 151–3
consumer-generated media *see* Web 2.0
consumer reviews 185–6, 187–91
cord-cutters 55, 60
corn seed 240–1
Covers.com 253
Craigslist 192, 201, 284
Crane, Richard 215
Crossing the Chasm (Moore) 242

DailyKos.com 62, 64
Dancing with the Stars 220–5, 236
data 10–11
privacy and 11–12
data arbitrage 218–39

real estate predictions 230–7
reality show predictions 220–7, 269–70
unemployment claims predictions 227–30
dating sites 34, 36, 124
Match.com 19
del.icio.us 172, 249, 254
demographics 11, 295, 296
depression 1–3
DeWolf, Chris 262–3
dieting and fitness 98–111, 114, 115, 122
The Biggest Loser and 106–7, 109, 118
diffusion of innovations 240–1, 245, 246, 248, 255, 256, 258
Digg 249, 254
domain and navigational searches 74–5, 201–2
domains
parked 20
squatting on 19
do-not-call lists 23, 54
drugs 3, 42
diet 110
erectile dysfunction 41, 42, 43–4
restless leg syndrome 280–1
smoking cessation 112
Dunbar, Robin 263, 266, 267
Dwinfour, Kofi 130–1

Early Adopters 60, 152–3, 194, 238, 239–58
Bohemian Mix 249, 250–1
Early Majority 241, 245, 247, 248, 256, 257
Money and Brains 249, 251–2
Young Digerati 59–60, 249, 253–4, 257
eBay 192, 201, 284
Ecast 174
Egotastic.com 132
80/20 rule 173–4, 193

email 71, 72, 84, 247
  market share of 181, 182
  spam 41–2, 43
  YouTube and 246–7
Encarta 169, 170–1
encyclopedias 169, 172
  Wikipedia *see* Wikipedia
engagement rings 94–6
E.T. 108
Expedia 184
Experian 189
Experience Project 152

Facebook 32, 36, 71, 110,
  179–83, 201, 239, 246, 251,
  265, 266, 282
Fall Out Boy 275–7
false hope syndrome 100, 102,
  105–6, 114
fan fiction 30
fashion industry 66, 258
  prom dresses and 89
fears 141–51
  of body parts 149–50
  of fear 150
  of long words 143–4
  of other cultures 150
  social 145–8, 150
  specific 149–51
  of subjects of study 150
  of unknown 151
Festinger, Leon 24
Flickr 171, 249, 254
  user participation in
    175–6
FOO camp 217, 226
Foster, Mike 27
Fox News 47, 48, 49
FoxNews.com 64
FreeRepublic 63
Friendster 36, 246, 257, 263,
  265–6, 267

Galaxy Search 18
gambling 25, 37–41

Early Adopters and 251,
  252–3, 254
  porn sites and 39
  restless leg syndrome drugs
    and 280–1
Game Neverending 171
Gawker 137
General Motors (GM) 203–10
Generation Next 71, 72
Gibson, Margaret 128–9
Gladwell, Malcolm 258, 264,
  269, 270, 282
glossary 295–6
Go Daddy 108–9, 253
Goldberg, Robert 6, 7
Golden Spruce 211, 213–16
*Golden Spruce, The: A True
  Story of Myth Madness and
  Greed*
  (Vaillant) 214
Google 17, 35, 154, 162, 202,
  239, 253–4
  MySpace outage and 34
  Orkut 251, 254–5
  Pontiac commercial 206–10
  Trends 59
  Video 167, 172
  Wikipedia and 212, 214
  YouTube and 247
Gross, Craig 27
Gross, Matt 27–8
Groundhog Day 186–7

Hershey Company 108
Hicks, Taylor 226
Hilton, Paris 121, 123–4, 134
Hilton, Perez 135–6 see also
  PerezHilton.com
Hindman, Matt 61–2
Hitwise Competitive
  Intelligence Service 4, 7–10,
  295
  methodology of 10–11
  privacy concerns and
    11–12

holidays
  Thanksgiving *see*
    Thanksgiving
  'why' questions about 161
home sales 230–7
Hopkins, Heather xiii, 13,
  269–70, 275
hotels 183–7
Hotels.com 186
Houran, Jim 124–5, 126, 134,
  138, 139
'how to' searches 109–10, 142,
  153–60
  on illicit or illegal activities
    159–60
  on sex 157, 159–60
  on tying a tie xiv, 156–7, 159
Huckabee, Mike 56, 64
Huffingtonpost.com 62, 64
Hurricane Katrina 96, 212, 213

IBM 52
  Consumer Digital Media
    Report 107
idea diffusion 239–41
imeem 251
information, perfect 186–7
innovations, diffusion of 240–1,
  245, 246, 248, 255, 256, 258
Innovative Marketing Summit
  50–1
Innovators 241–2, 246, 247,
  248
instant gratification 110, 119
In-Stat 55
International Formal
  Association (IFA) 97
Irwin, Steve 130, 131
ISPs 10–11

Jackson, Janet 108
January
  depression in 1
  erectile dysfunction drug
    searches in 44

New Year's resolutions in 83,
  97–105, 109, 111–19
prom dress searches in 73–88,
  118–19
wedding dress searches in 94,
  118–19
Jennings, Peter 113
Judaism 163–4
Juran, Joseph 173, 174
JustJared 133

Kaplan, Shel 218
Kapor, Mitch 218
Karim, Jawed 245
Kayak 186
Kazaa 244
Keibler, Stacy 221–5
Kremen, Gary 18–21
Kushner, Harold 164

Labor, U.S. Department of 227,
  228, 230
Lachey, Drew 222–5
Laggards 241
Landon, Alf 45–6
Larson, Sarah 133
Late Majority 241
'Lazy Sunday,' 248
Legacy.com 284
Lenovo 50–1, 52–3
Literary Digest 45, 54, 55, 67
Long Tail, The (Anderson) 174
LookSmart 5–10, 18, 19
Lotus Development
    Corporation 218
Ludicorp 171
lung cancer 112, 113–14
lurkers 174–5
Lycos 239

McCain, Edwin 72
McCain, John 56
McCain, Meghan 68
McConaughey, Matthew 133
McCutcheon and Lange 124

McIntyre, Joey 221
MacKenzie, D. W. 186
McPhee, Katharine 226
magazines 65–6, 89
Maher, Chris 4, 7, 9
Mapquest 201
market research surveys 22–4, 25, 26, 44, 46–7, 53, 54–6, 67, 76, 84, 210
  Do-Not-Call Registry and 54
market share 296
MarketWatch.com 252
Mars 108
Marshall, J. Howard 128
Match.com 19
Mazda 208–9
Meakings, Oliver 90
Michaels, Jillian 106
Michelle, Candice 108–9
Microsoft 17
  Encarta 169, 170–1
  Facebook and 180
  see also MSN Search
Mirapex 280
mobile-phone-only homes 54–6
Mobissimo 186
Monaco, Kelly 221
Money and Brains segment 249, 251–2
Montag, Heidi 68
Moore, Geoffrey 242
Mortality 128
MOSAIC segmentation system 189, 190, 296
Motorola 168
MSN Search 7, 9, 210, 231, 239
musical bands and artists
  Arctic Monkeys 259–62, 270–2
  Fall Out Boy 275–7
  MySpace and 272–3, 274, 275, 277
  tipping point for 270–7
Muslims 163
MySpace 32, 35, 168, 179, 200, 201, 239, 246, 251, 266, 282

Arctic Monkeys and 271
  'Cassie' persona on 81–2
  launching of 262–3
  music and 272–3, 274, 275, 277
  outage on 32–3
  'Taylor' persona on 70–81, 86
  Tequila and 263, 266–7, 268

National Association of Realtors (NAR) 230, 231, 232, 234, 235
National Comorbidity Survey 141–2, 143, 145
National Institute of Mental Health 146
navigational searches 74–5, 201–2, 247
NBC 106, 109, 248
NBC.com 215–16
neckties xiv, 155–7
news 192–4, 284–5
  political bias and 64
newspaper industry 192–4, 284–5
New Year's resolutions 83, 97–105, 109, 111–19
New Yorker, The 188, 264
Nielsen, Jakob 174–5, 176, 193
Nielsen Company 77
9/11 95–6
Norris, Chuck 56
NYTimes.com 251

Obama, Barack 47–9, 53, 56, 67, 68, 139
obituaries 192, 284
Official Women of Wrestling 225
ofoto.com 171
O'Hurley, John 221
1-9-90 rule 174–5, 176–7, 193
Online Publishers Association 85
opt-in data 11
O'Reilly, Tim 217

Orkut 251, 254–5
Overstock.com 238

Page, Larry 217
Palin, Sarah xiv, xv, 67–8
Pants-Off Dance-Off 267
Pareto, Vilfredo 173
Pareto Principle 172–3, 193
Parnell, Chris 248
Paul, Ron 58–60
PerezHilton.com 122, 133, 134,
    135–7, 192–3
perfect information 186–7
Pew Internet Group 167
phobias see fears
photo sharing 171–2
    on Flickr 171, 175–6, 249, 254
Pinnacle Sports 223
politics 44, 45–50, 55–64
    Barack Obama 47–9, 53, 56, 67,
        68, 139
    bias in coverage and audience
        of 64
    blogs and 61–4, 192
    predicting election outcomes
        45–7, 55, 57–8, 60, 63–4
    Ron Paul 58–60
Polivy, Janet 100, 102
Pontiac G6 206–10
Pontiac Solstice 203–6
pornography sites 17–36
    age demographic and 34
    celebrity sex tapes 126, 127
    regional breakdown of visitors
        to 31–2
    visits to gambling sites
        compared with 39
    women's visits to and
        involvement in 29–30
Porn Sunday 27
PostSecret (Warren) 151
PPC (pay per click) 13
predictions
    arbitrage vs. 219 see also data
        arbitrage

of election outcomes 45–7, 55,
    57–8, 60, 63–4
pregnancy 83, 114–18
Pregnancy.org 116–17, 118
Prescott, LeeAnn 94, 142–3
privacy 11–12
PRIZM segmentation system
    77, 81, 129, 137, 249, 296
product placement 107–8, 203–6
prom 69–93, 119
    in United Kingdom 90–3
Propeller.com 132
psychographics 11, 296

Ramprakash, Mark 269
Real Clear Politics 63
real estate 230–7
Reese's Pieces 108
Reeve, Christopher 113
Reeve, Dana 113–14
religion 27–9, 163–4
    Obama and 47–9
Requip 281
restless leg syndrome (RLS)
    280–1
restaurant reviews 188, 190–1
Rice, Jerry 222–5
Richie, Nicole 123
Rogers, Everett 241–2, 245, 246,
    256
Roosevelt, Franklin 45–6
Rule of 150 263, 266, 267
Ryan, Bryce 240–1, 282

Samberg, Andy 248
Sanford Bernstein 108
Saturday Night Live 248
Search, The (Battelle) 200
Search Engine Strategies
    Conference 197–200
searches
    domain and navigational 74–5,
        201–2, 247
    number of words in 203
    volume of 296

for week of 15 December 2007 200–1

Wikipedia and 211–15

search-term breadth 296

search-term data 11

search-term suggestion report 224

SEOs (search-engine optimizers) 208

SERP (search engine result page) 207–8

sex.com 19–21

sex searches 35
  'how to ' 157, 159–60
  see also pornography sites

sex tapes, celebrity 126, 127

SFGate.com 251

Simmons, Gene 131

Simmons, Russell 189

Simonsen, Michael 218–19

Simple Life, The 123

small world phenomenon (six degrees of separation) 264

Smith, Anna Nicole 121, 122, 127–30

smoking cessation 112–14, 115

social fears 145–8, 150

social networks 70, 179–83, 201, 256, 258, 263–9
  dating sites *see* dating sites
  del.icio.us 172, 249, 254
  Digg 249, 254
  Early Adopters and 251
  Facebook 32, 36, 71, 110, 179–83, 201, 239, 246, 251, 265, 266, 282
  Flickr 171, 175–6, 249, 254
  Friendster 36, 246, 257, 263, 265–6, 267
  market share of 181
  MySpace *see* MySpace
  Orkut 251, 254–5
  participation 174–5
  pornography and 32–6

video-sharing *see* videosharing sites

webcam-based 256

YouTube and 246–7

spam email 41–2, 43

Spears, Britney 162

specific fears 149–51

Spielberg, Steven 108

Stacy Keibler Correction Coefficient (SKCC) 225, 237

Stark, Philip 17

Steiner, Peter 188

Stickam.com 256

Stoppelman, Jeremy 189

streaming videos 255

Strictly Come Dancing 226, 269

Super Bowl 44, 108–9

swimwear 104

tagging 172

Tatham, Matt 234

Telepictures Productions 137

television 107
  commercials on 44, 102, 107, 206–10
  predicting reality show winners 220–7, 269–70
  product placement in 107–8, 203–6

Tequila, Tila 263, 266–7, 268

term volume 225

Thanksgiving 161
  depression and 1–3
  dieting and 103, 105, 107
  engagement rings and 94–5

TheStreet.com 252

ThinkPad 51–2

TIME 5, 36, 154, 180

TIME.com 153

timing 69, 96

Tipping Point, The (Gladwell) 258, 264, 265, 269

tipping point for music artists online 270–7

TMZ.com 122, 134, 137

Tonioli, Bruno 221
travel and hospitality industry 183–9
Treasure Hunters 215–16
TripAdvisor.com 9, 184–5, 187, 188, 252
Trojan horses 42
True 124
Truemomconfessions.com 152
Turner, Alex 260
Tweed, Shannon 131
Twitter 71, 110

un-conference movement 217
unemployment claims 227–30
United Kingdom xii–xv
  'how to tie a tie' searches in xiv, 156
  prom in 90–3
University of Toronto 100
USA Today 226
user visits 296

Vaillant, John 214
Vann-Adib, Robbie 174
Veoh 255
vertical search 200
Viagra 41–2
video-sharing sites 255, 258
  Bix 256
  Google 167, 172
  Yahoo! 172, 244, 245
  YouTube *see* YouTube
viral marketing 168
volume of searches 296

Wales, Jimmy 169, 218
Walmart 201
Warren, Frank 151
Wastler, Allen 59, 60
Web 2.0 167–94, 243, 261
  social networks in *see* social networks
  travel industry and 183–9
  user participation in 172–9

Web 3.0 191–2
webcam-based social networks 256
Webcamnow.com 256
weddings 7, 8, 93–4, 96, 114, 118–19, 157
Weisberg, Lois 264–5, 266, 268
Wells, Jane 234–5
When Prophecy Fails (Festinger) 24
'why' searches 160–5
  on relationships 162
  on religion 163–4
Wikimedia Commons 255
Wikipedia 169–71, 172, 211–12, 218
  top ten search terms leading to 211–15
  user participation in 175–8
Winfrey, Oprah 136, 138–9

Xanga 246
Xdrive 262
xxxchurch.com 27

Yahoo! 201
  Bix 256
  Mail 182
  Search 154, 210, 239
  Video 172, 244, 245
Yelp.com 189, 191
Young Contemporaries segment 189–90, 191
Young Digerati segment 59–60, 249, 253–4, 257
YouTube 172, 201, 239, 254, 256, 265
  growth of 243–9, 251
  user participation in 175–9